D1008050

THE STAKES OF THIS NO-NAME BATTLE WERE SIMPLE. WIN OR DIE.

Hooper tossed in a grenade and then scrambled to the next enemy bunker in line, repeating the process before moving on to a third. One by one, the grenades blew behind him.

Rising black clouds of debris, swirling dirt, and an invisible wave of intense heat from the explosions followed him as he ran, the glowing splinters of metal fragments from secondary explosions tearing into his back and legs. Small holes and spreading rosettes of blood mottled his jungle fatigues. The pain spread like needles in his brain. Where the shrapnel didn't penetrate his skin, it burned red welts.

Hooper was a mess. He was covered with dirt, soot from the gunsmoke, and his and others' blood. Still, charging forward, Hooper looked like a demon. The fighting was growing more hectic and confusing, and the NVA soldiers were charging out to attack, only to be cut down short of their intended targets—most of the time.

In other moments, grisly hand-to-hand combat scenes were being played out in grunting, swearing, life-and-death struggles. . . .

By Kregg P. J. Jorgenson

ACCEPTABLE LOSS: *An Infantry Soldier's Perspective*
MIA RESCUE: *LRRPs in Cambodia*
LRRP COMPANY COMMAND: *The Cav's LRP/Rangers in Vietnam, 1968–1969*
VERY CRAZY, G.I.: *Strange but True Stories of the Vietnam War*

Books published by The Random House Publishing Group are available at quantity discounts on bulk purchases for premium, educational, fund-raising, and special sales use. For details, please call 1-800-733-3000.

VERY CRAZY, G.I.

Strange but True Stories of the Vietnam War

Kregg P. J. Jorgenson

PRESIDIO PRESS · NEW YORK

Sale of this book without a front cover may be unauthorized. If this book is coverless, it may have been reported to the publisher as "unsold or destroyed" and neither the author nor the publisher may have received payment for it.

A Presidio Press Book
Published by The Random House Publishing Group
Copyright © 2001 by Kregg P. J. Jorgenson

All rights reserved.

Published in the United States by Presidio Press, an imprint of The Random House Publishing Group, a division of Random House, Inc., New York, and simultaneously in Canada by Random House of Canada Limited, Toronto. Portions of this book originally appeared in *Beaucoup Dinky Dau,* published by Maxwell James Publishing, Seattle, Washington, in 1994. Copyright © 1994 by Kregg P. J. Jorgenson. "Dead Reckoning," "A Good Ambush," "'I Killed Ho Chi Ming,'" and "Lions and Tigers and Flares, Oh My!" first appeared in *Behind the Lines* magazine while "The *Nguoi Rung*" and "Ripples and Waves" appeared in BTL World–On Line.

Presidio Press and colophon are trademarks of Random House, Inc.

www.presidiopress.com

Library of Congress Catalog Card Number: 00-109141

ISBN 0-8041-1598-2

Manufactured in the United States of America

First Edition: February 2001

To Doc L. Wayne Ball, a veteran of the war stories and medic for their casualties, with thanks for the service and the belief that the stories matter.

There are more things in heaven and earth, Horatio, than are dreamt of in your philosophy.

—WILLIAM SHAKESPEARE

CONTENTS

ACKNOWLEDGMENTS

I'd like to thank or acknowledge the following people for their contributions to this project: the late Joe Hooper, for his service in Vietnam and his service with the Veterans Administration in Seattle, Washington. Besides his official duties, in the seventies, Hooper spoke to many service groups, schools, and colleges in the Pacific Northwest and, although he wasn't always well received during those difficult times, the quiet, unassuming veteran offered his unique insight and reflections on a war that a nation no longer had time for. Over coffee, Joe Hooper was often candid but never boastful. His story has been re-created from the official record, the recollections of several of his close friends, a *Stars and Stripes* newspaper account, and from comments by Hooper himself.

In this regard, I also need to thank Gary Linderer, executive editor at *Behind the Lines* magazine, for his help in tracking down both the official and unofficial record of Sgt. Joe Hooper, and for the introduction to Derby Jones and Rey Martinez, friends of Hooper, who provided a personal view and human side to one of the nation's most decorated and forgotten heroes. I also have to give a nod to my brother, Keith B. Jorgenson, who provided his own insight to Hooper from their extensive conversations at Highline Community College.

Thanks also go to retired Marine Sgt. Maj. James P. Henderson for his input on the United States Marine Corps and his special-flavor "war stories." Henderson's colorful accounts and commentary might cause a few of the more timid readers to pause or even blush, but they offer a realistic view of the war that words like *darn* and *shucks* just don't convey. Henderson's delivery only adds to the telling. I'm proud to be in his company. Former Marine Luis Sanchez also gets a loud "Semper fi" for his help, as do several other former Leathernecks who prefer to remain anonymous.

From the Veterans of Foreign Wars, Chapter 2886, in Federal Way, Washington, I'd like to salute Richard Keeton, Don Hulslander, Darrell Pilat, Greg Westmiller, and the rest of the members, for their stories, their service and sincerity, and of course, their coffee. These are veterans who continue to aid their service organization and communities with admirable effort and commitment.

One of the more unique sightings of something unusual during the war comes from Craig Thompson of Olympia, Washington. Thompson, a former paratrooper with the 173d Airborne, provided not only the story but interesting proof.

For the air force assistance, I thank Ron Jacobson and J. Patrick Kelly, who provided technical data on B-52s and their payloads and things that fly in general, how they fly, and why they're always good to have on your side in a conflict.

I need to acknowledge the late John Sarten, who was a genuine character, for his encouragement over the years. I suspect that everyone who had the pleasure of knowing him enjoyed his wit, wisdom, and abundant humor. The rascally old retired navy chief petty officer was a true storyteller and is sorely missed.

From the Vietnam Veterans of America, Chapter 318

of Albuquerque, New Mexico, thanks specifically to the late Doug Cochrane for his assistance concerning his brother, Deverton. Former 1st Cav LRRP/Ranger Frank Duggan gets a nod too for offering the irony to the account "Namesake." Duggan now makes his home in the Virgin Islands, where he proudly displays his 75th Ranger Scroll over the bar in his restaurant, Duggan's Reef.

Thanks, too, go to David Willson (author of *The REMF* and *The REMF Revisited*) for his perspective and his work educating college students on the subject of the Vietnam war. Willson teaches several courses, including one relating to the war and the media. He frequently hosts forums for Vietnam veteran writers, and if there is a more well-read veteran, anywhere, on the subject of the Vietnam War, he or she will find Willson a fellow scholar.

I'd like to thank Bill McIntosh, a former scout pilot with the 1st of the 9th Cav (1st Air Cavalry Division), for his contribution. Mini-Mac was a remarkable pilot whose war story takes place on the ground.

I need to thank Rangers Robert Edward Beal, Grover "Gene" Sprague, Bob "Moose" McClure, Danny Pope, Kenn Miller, Riley "Dozer" Cox and his wife Linda, James W. "Limey" Walker, Cmd. Sgt. Maj. (ret.) Tony Cortez; Special Forces veterans Raymond Garofalo, Sgt. Maj. (ret.) John Larsen, and so many others who gave so much with no expectation in return. Finally, I need to thank my wife, Katherine, for her patience and the support needed to complete this project. In the hubbub and confusion, I'm sure I've overlooked others who were equally helpful with this project, and for this oversight, I apologize and offer my sincere appreciation.

PREFACE

"Beaucoup dinky dau" is a slang G.I. expression, a bastardization of French and Vietnamese, that American G.I.'s during the Vietnam War knew meant "very crazy," a term that I think most readers will agree is appropriate for the things that occur in this collection of unusual stories and oddities.

The stories found in the following pages are that and more. They are some of the strange and unique accounts I collected during my tenure as a senior editor at *Behind the Lines* magazine and as a columnist for various military-related publications.

Although all of the stories are alleged to be true, there are a few even I think are far-fetched, perhaps even suspect. However, having said that, I must add that when several of the more unusual stories first appeared in print, I received candid calls from other veterans who claimed similar things had happened to them, which is why I'll leave it to the reader to sift and sort through the stories and to make up his or her own mind as to what to believe. It was Col. Harry Summers, founder of *Vietnam Magazine* and one of the best-regarded historians of the Vietnam War, who pointed out that there were "thousands of truths" in the war. This collection of stories almost certainly offers several more.

Where I can, I have used the real names, units, and

other pertinent information in the retelling. In some instances, at the request of veterans involved, I've changed names, unit designations, locations, and dates to protect their privacy for reasons that will make themselves evident as their stories unfold. Anonymity has its place and value.

Perhaps the obvious question is "Why another book on the Vietnam War?" With all of the books, news reports, films, and documentaries on the war, anyone would think everything has been covered by now. Unfortunately, given the stereotypes and prejudices current about the war and those caught up in it, there's room for a few more stories that might shine some light on the subject and take us into a new realm of understanding. And, too, there are probably even a few more surprises for us all. Vietnam is still a nation of surprises.

For example, late in 1992, a team of scientists exploring a remote stretch of rugged jungle mountains on the border with Laos made a startling zoological find. In ancient rain forests, they discovered a large, previously unknown mammal, a forest goat to be specific (named *sao lo* in Vietnamese, for the weaving spindlelike horns). The *sao lo* stood three feet tall and weighed over two hundred pounds. What's more, the scientists discovered several new species of exotic bird and a never-before-seen yellow-shell turtle.

No big thing, right? Just odd and unusual wildlife?

Well, think about it for a moment. On the surface, the discoveries may not sound like much, but it is something amazing because, for two thousand years, Vietnam has been involved in on-again, off-again wars with the Chinese, Khmers, the French, Japanese, the Americans and their allies, Cambodians, and others. In the twentieth century alone, there have been myriad raids and reconnaissance missions, shellings, massive bomb runs, storms of chemical defoliants rained over the forests, and constant monitoring from spy planes, sensitive listening devices, and satellites from space that were capable of photographing the serial numbers of enemy vehicles. Despite all that, the unique goat, birds, turtles, and—more than likely—other animals went unnoticed.

It took a few intrepid field zoologists to push back the branches and shed some new light on things that weren't supposed to have been there.

After thirty-plus years, some of us are still trying to learn more about the war we thought we already knew and understood. Like the zoologists, we're still pushing back the brush and tangled branches, still making accidental discoveries that frighten, amuse, surprise, or even amaze us. With a little fieldwork of our own, we're finding new ways to view or interpret what happened in order to get a better understanding of ourselves and of people and things *we* stereotype.

Why? Because sometimes what we think we know has little at all to do with truth, let alone fact. We've just accepted something without question until it has become part of our collective knowledge or lore.

Take the word *kangaroo,* for instance. When the English first encountered one of the large marsupials hopping around the land Down Under, they were startled and astounded by the strange creature and asked one of the aborigines who accompanied them what it was.

"Kangaroo?" was the reply.

"Kangaroo! Splendid!" echoed the English, and the name stuck and became part of our historical lexicon. It was history, zoology, and hopping misunderstanding, too, for that matter, because in the dialect of the aborigines *kangaroo* means something akin to "I'm not certain what you're asking."

The Englishman hadn't made himself clear so the

reply to his question, and its interpretation, became a simple misunderstanding, one we've all come to accept. The English aren't alone.

Remember the fight scenes in the gladiator movies where the thumbs-up or thumbs-down gesture is given by the emperor to the victorious fighter? Well, from a Vatican scholar, I learned there was a basis in fact for the gestures; however, there is an interesting twist.

From the movies, we see that the thumbs-up sign means "Let him live!" while the thumbs-down sign means "Kill him!"

Sort of.

Actually, the historical technical adviser explained the gestures to the movie people, what they meant and when they were used. But when it came time to shoot the scene, someone confused the two gestures. In fact, the thumbs-up sign meant "Send him to the gods!"—that is, "Kill him!"—and the thumbs-down gesture meant "Let him remain on earth." It is ironic that today movie critics use the confused thumbs-up and thumbs-down gestures to judge the latest Hollywood releases.

I think it was Ernest Hemingway who, after a life of chasing wars and his own demons by placing himself in myriad conflicts and dangers, came away convinced that all fact is fiction and all fiction is fact, that little in life—in his life anyway—was what it seemed. Although I didn't quite understand what that meant before I went off to the army and to the Vietnam War, the observation took on more depth and meaning upon my return. As did the words of the American author and humorist Mark Twain, who said, "Why shouldn't truth be stranger than fiction? After all, fiction has to make sense!"

Twain well understood the complexities and absurdities of real life. With his stories and insight, he taught us how to better look and laugh at ourselves and at the pomp and pageantry we sometimes resort to in order to hide our worst failings and fears.

Real life, at least the "civilized" variety, often confounded him, as did the little and large mysteries and unexplained behavior, which only added to his skepticism and belief that not everything can be neatly packaged or labeled.

The same, too, can be said of the American war in Vietnam. Much of what we've learned of the war and what prejudices we hold need to be reexamined and reviewed as we struggle to make some sense of the turmoil of those years and to learn from the ordeal. It is a long process of examination and reexamination to find meaning, value, and closure.

Like the zoologists, we, too, need to push back a few more leaves and branches and do more fieldwork. The difficulty in any exploration comes in trying to keep an open mind about what we discover and what we label.

There are no lectures here, just stories that will help you get a better understanding of the American war in Vietnam from some of the people who did the fieldwork.

Kregg P. J. Jorgenson

Republic of Vietnam

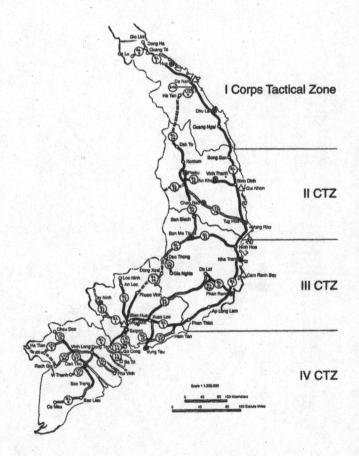

I Corps Tactical Zone

II CTZ

III CTZ

IV CTZ

Scale 1:1,250,000

DEAD RECKONING

Perhaps one of the deadliest threats to anyone stationed in Vietnam during the war came from Viet Cong or North Vietnamese Army mortar or Katyusha 122mm-rocket artillery fire. At any moment and, seemingly, any facility, the "incoming" (as it was better known) could rain down and wound or kill anyone within its deadly radius. In this story, you'll come to better understand another aspect of that frightening reality and, too, the terror of getting hit.

In war, you will die like a dog for no good reason.
—ERNEST HEMINGWAY

Dong Ha, Vietnam

The North Vietnamese Army's Van An Rocket Artillery Regiment had it in for the Marine 3d Recon Battalion. At least, at times, it felt that way. The base camp at Dong Ha seemed to be one of their favorite target areas and, too, maybe one of their easiest.

Dong Ha was located on Highway 9, less than ten miles from the DMZ in the I Corps Military Region, the

1

northernmost of the four corps tactical zones into which Vietnam was divided. The DMZ was the infamous and misnamed Demilitarized Zone that separated North Vietnam from South Vietnam, and it was anything but *de*militarized. The North Vietnamese Army used it as a springboard for attacks in I Corps, and since their rocket artillery rounds could easily cover the distance, Dong Ha was not only a target of choice for the NVA artillery gunners but a target of opportunity as well.

This time, they were walking the Russian 122mm rockets into the base with such precision that even the uninitiated could see it wasn't a random attack. The deafening explosions of the forty-pound warheads erupted in an evident pattern as specific sites were being targeted. With their vast spy network throughout the region, the Communist gunners knew the Marine facility well and took full advantage of the knowledge.

However, even before the first rocket slammed into the tents or tin-roofed barracks hootches, and split seconds before the base camp's warning siren began building into a screaming wail, Sgt. James P. Henderson recognized their distinctive *whoosh*, like a truck's tires at high speed on a wet road, for what it was and yelled at his people to get to the protective sandbagged bunkers outside.

"Incoming!" the wiry noncommissioned officer yelled, pulling Marines out of the barracks and shoving them toward the nearest bunker, just around the corner of the hootch. "Go! Go! Go!"

The rockets were falling in rapid succession, dancing across the base in deadly, macabre steps. *Whoomph*s followed the screaming *whoosh*es and the thundering roars of secondary explosions that told of direct hits. Hot shrapnel rained across the camp, ripping and tearing through anything and anyone in its way.

Rising black plumes and the acrid, oily odor of burning fuel confirmed the NVA gunners' accuracy. Since the bases and camps were stationary, the ranges had long been defined and plotted by the Viet Cong and NVA. Besides, they'd had years of practice.

Another 122mm rocket slammed into the next hootch over, tearing through the sheet-metal roofing and gutting the wood-frame building.

Someone was screaming for a corpsman, then the call was drowned out by still another series of *whoomph*s and explosions. The impacts and detonations sent tremors across the base.

His rifle in hand, Henderson grabbed his flak jacket and steel-pot helmet and took off in a dead run, following the others. If a ground attack followed, he would damn well be ready. The North Vietnamese Army sometimes attempted a ground assault after a shelling, hoping that the Americans' defenses had been weakened or were inadequately manned.

Henderson had just turned the corner of his hootch and was within a few feet of the bunker's opening when a rocket exploded a few yards behind him. The blast slammed into his back, and the intense heat, splintered metal, and concussion lifted him up off the ground forcefully and threw him down limply like a discarded doll.

The pain was intense and overwhelming, and when Henderson tried to lift himself up and turn over, his arms and legs wouldn't respond. They couldn't. There was too much weight on his legs and back. Lying facedown in the hard-packed orange earth, he wondered what had fallen on top of him. Building debris, most likely. But why was it so heavy?

His breaths were shallow, and he was soon struggling for air, fighting a dark current that threatened to sweep up and overpower him. His chest burned, and the air that somehow squeezed through to his lungs only fanned his pain. In the distance, someone was yelling for a corpsman, but the voice seemed too far away to matter. He knew he was hurt, but he couldn't determine how badly. What was on his back?

He couldn't see any debris, but then he couldn't focus either; every time he opened his eyes, a searing light burned through his sockets. It was too bright and blinding to let anything else in. Then, in an instant, the light began to fade, and a shadowy world took its place around him. He was fading into black.

Most of his hearing was lost, and what sound filtered through was muffled by the blood he could feel flowing from his ears. He would learn later that his eardrums were shattered. Between the shaking from the follow-up explosions and the cool shuddering earth, he could feel the burning pain of his broken body.

Something was flowing down the side of his face and spilling into his mouth. The droplets tasted like warm copper droplets, and memory recognized it instantly. It was blood. He wanted to spit it out but couldn't even find the strength to do that. Instead, he managed to use his tongue to push it through his lips, and it dribbled to the ground. He could feel it pool in the soil beneath his cheek.

When he tried to call for help nothing came out. The shallow exhaled breaths didn't allow words, and in a terrible, frightening instant, he understood his fate. He was dying.

Panic began to take over, but it was too late for that, too. The shadows grew darker, and the pain lessened, drifting off, actually leaving him in the cold tide of darkness.

All around him, the rain of rockets fell, then finally danced off to another part of the base. Through the earth, he felt their rumble diminish, moving away in big, labored steps.

Moments later, it was still. Too still.

For what seemed like an eternity, there was nothing for Henderson. No sudden rush of life's reruns or regrets. Nothing but white noise and an internal pounding that replaced the exploding artillery rounds. The internal pounding was his pulse, and he could sense that the beats were lessening.

Then he still couldn't see, but he could feel someone at his side gently turning him over, and he heard a yell, "Over here! Head wound!" The Marine sergeant could barely hear the other wounded and dying Marines crying around him, but that was enough to bring back the panic.

"I can't get a pulse! Don't die on me, you son of a bitch!" he heard that someone say as though in the distance, and although Henderson couldn't see the Marine shaking his head wearily or see the man's blood-drenched hands, he could sense what was happening next as the man lowered him back to the ground. "Ah, Christ!" the man said, distant and faint.

"Don't go! I'm not dead!" Henderson yelled in his mind, only no one else could hear. The back of his head was broken open where rocket shrapnel had pushed his steel pot back into his skull like a baseball shattering a window.

James P. Henderson's world and life were bleeding away, swirling steadily toward a small opening of light propped against a dark sea backdrop. He was being sucked into a whirlpool, and he fought it until there was no choice but to spiral with it; he didn't have the strength, and he realized it with a reluctant acceptance. He wouldn't go easily, but he was going. Within seconds, he was gone.

Dead.

Killed In Action.

Sergeant James P. Henderson's body was loaded into the olive drab rubber body bag, zipped in with finality, and placed alongside the others killed in the rocket attack. The line of Marines killed in action was growing steadily as, one by one, the body bags and ponchos used as makeshift body bags were brought into quiet formation. Other survivors stood around, dazed and stunned by the bloody scene. Some were lighting cigarettes with shaking hands, hoping that the smoke would curb the stench of dead comrades whose bodies were already bloating beneath the hot Vietnamese sun.

Their eyes showed the beginnings of survivor's guilt and the shame that came with feeling glad, *really* glad, that it was someone else and not them. These were their buddies, their fellow Marines, and death didn't really give a damn.

The overworked navy corpsman yelled for assistance while loading the wounded into commandeered jeeps and trucks, and his call was amplified by a gunnery sergeant who took charge and brought the survivors back to the task at hand.

"Let's go, people!" the gunny said, raising his voice to get their attention and pull them out of their own distant thoughts. "We need a hand over here!"

The Marines moved more quickly as they helped the wounded. Those who could not walk were assisted by survivors better off, and there was no shortage of help.

It was only later, after all of the wounded had been taken to the field hospital, that the corpsman turned his attention back to the line of body bags and the dead Marines. It was the part of his job he hated more than anything and why he hated Vietnam and the fucking war.

He sighed audibly, looking over the bloodied body bags. He shook his head and swore. When he was ready, he went to work. One by one, he worked his way down the solemn row, unzipping each body bag, removing the dead Marine's dog tags, and swearing again when he turned the dead Marine's head back to face him. The Marine was maybe all of nineteen or twenty years old with dumb fucking Opie of Mayberry red hair, freckles, and green eyes, and a hole in his chest the size of a soft-ball. His heart and lungs were blown through his back.

The corpsman wedged one of the dog tags between the dead man's teeth and hit it with the butt of his K-bar knife to lodge it in place. He took the other and placed it in his utility jacket pocket to turn over to the platoon leader when the grisly job was done.

It was standard operating procedure, SOP for the task, part of it anyway. The rest dictated that the corpsman would punch a hole in the dead marine's ear with a handheld hole punch and attach a twist-tie card containing the necessary information about the dead Marine so the Graves Registration people could process the remains Stateside.

The corpsman twist-tied the wire attached to the card twice so it wouldn't dislodge from the dead man's body in transit. Bloodied rubber body bags. Envelopes, really, that would eventually become dead letters home.

The corpsman zipped the bag back up and went on to the next one in line and the next and the next.

"Henderson, James P., Sergeant," the corpsman said to himself, reading the fifth dead Marine's dog tag. A dark wet and sticky maroon pool mushroomed across the back of Henderson's utility uniform. Bits and pieces of severed flesh clung to the side of the body bag and fell on the corpsman's forearms as he reached in to turn the dead man's head.

"Shit!" he said, despising what he was doing. He'd been trained to save people, not process them like meat. He struggled to lodge the dog tag in place and absent-mindedly dropped the second tag into his pocket with the others. Reaching back in with the hole punch, he worked the metal lips into the soft flesh of Henderson's ear and pressed both handles together, creating a path for the information card. Only just as the hole punch made the hole, the Marine sergeant rose up slightly and said "Hello!" to the stunned medic, who quickly dropped the dead Marine and crab-scrambled back away from the body bag.

His heart was thumping wildly in his chest just as it had done when he was nine and someone had jumped out of the dark and screamed, "Boo!" He was breathing rapidly, and he was genuinely scared; the dead don't talk and they sure as hell don't sit up and say, "Hello!" Henderson, James P., Sergeant, was still alive!

"Get me some help over here!" the corpsman yelled, rushing back to the Marine in the body bag. Throwing his ear against the dead man's chest, he yelled again. "Get me some help over here! Now! This one's still alive!"

Placing his fingers on the carotid artery on Henderson's bloody neck, the corpsman found a pulse. The faint beat was barely registering, but it was there. A pulse!

The corpsman was yelling again to a bewildered audience who had gathered around the medic. "Get a jeep! He's still alive!" Then, turning back to Henderson and cradling the man, he added, "Hang in there, Sarge.

You're going to make it. You hear me? Damn it! You're going to make it!"

Weeks later, awake and recovering in a cool, clean military hospital thousands of miles from the war, Henderson, James P., Sergeant, was beginning to learn more of the details of what had happened and what had almost happened. The specifics left the Marine sergeant more than a little uncomfortable and unnerved.

The physical recovery was slow. His vision had returned, as had some of his hearing, but he was still having difficulty speaking. The rocket's explosion had shattered the back of his skull and a metal plate had been inserted there to strengthen the area. His memory was coming back, but it wasn't all there yet.

Shrapnel had broken ribs and littered his body from his back down to his feet. He was a mess, but he was alive. With enough physical therapy and time, he'd bounce back. He'd have scars, plates, and shrapnel fragments as reminders.

When the hospital commander came by to award him a Purple Heart, the officer asked if there was anything he could do for him. Henderson nodded and reached for the pencil and paper that he used for communication until his speech returned fully.

Scribbling out a note, he handed it to the naval medical officer, who read it, smiled, and nodded his response.

"Can do, Sergeant," the hospital commander added, reading the handwritten note over again and stifling a laugh. "I'll take care of it for you personally."

The hospital commander laughed again at the Marine sergeant's note, pocketing it as he walked off the ward. The note read: "I guess I was so busy being dead, I forgot my manners, sir. Please find out the corpsman's name who decided I didn't need to go to hell just yet and buy him a case of whatever he drinks. Charge it to me, and tell the squid thanks."

James P. Henderson retired as a command sergeant major after thirty-two years with the United States Marine Corps. In some circles, a command sergeant major ranks up there on Olympus next to Zeus as a secondary god of thunder.

However, before his long climb to the top of the enlisted ranks, Henderson spent his time on the line, serving nearly four tours of duty in Vietnam. In his forty-four months of combat service, J. P. Henderson earned a Silver Star for gallantry, a Bronze Star for heroism, six Purple Hearts, five significant single-mission Air Medals, twenty Air Medal Mission awards, the Navy Commendation Medal, and various other awards and decorations.

He also successfully completed the United States Army's Ranger and parachute training and a number of other service special warfare–related schools. A former Marine and, perhaps, a Marine's Marine, James P. Henderson is a law-enforcement officer in southern California.

THE EVIL GOD

The battle for good and evil takes many twists and turns in combat, and the definitions a soldier comes away with afterward depend largely upon the belief system he brought with him and the god or gods he serves. The following story will introduce you to a new belief system and offer a closer look at an evil god.

Religions are born and may die, but superstition is immortal. Only the fortunate can take life without mythology.
—WILL AND ARIEL DURANT

It was an ancient farming practice. The tribal hill people, the montagnards, were using slash-and-burn techniques in a portion of the jungle to plant their spring crops. The planting and harvesting of crops were a necessary part of their survival, and while they went about their daily lives in a war zone, the unseen dangers were never all that far away.

A deadly cobra, driven out of its nest by a wall of rising flames, struck out from the roiling black smoke and bit an old man whose attention was focused on the fire. The mud-brown snake pumped its venom into the old man, then slithered away into the jungle while the villagers quickly came to the man's aid. The old man had been bitten in the thigh, the wounds too close to or in the femoral artery.

"Poor bastard," said a veteran Special Forces master sergeant to no one in particular when he had heard what had happened to the old man. More than likely, the snakebite victim had been carried back to the village and into a large communal hut. There the man would prepare to die. His grieving family had probably already said their good-byes, while the village shaman would do what he could to help ease his suffering.

Soon the old man would slip into a venom-induced coma, his respiratory system would shut down, and he would die. There was no antivenom in the remote camp for a cobra's deadly bite, and there was nothing anyone could do to stop the old man from dying, not the American army medic nor even the suspicious village shaman, who knew the real cause was something far more sinister.

Malaria or dysentery had claimed three of the tribe's children over the preceding months and plagued the adult population, and although the Special Forces advisers had medicines and malaria tablets flown in to help combat the problem, the shaman knew the problem was more than the mosquitoes or fouled water.

And when the young mother who was bathing her baby in the mud-brown stream nearby let out a frightening scream as she was brutally attacked and then dragged off into the jungle, the shaman knew for certain what it was and gave name to his suspicions.

"*Kanam,*" he whispered, as the rescuers gathered on the stream bank, cradled their weapons, and stared at the bloody trail leading into the rain forest. As the old man's soft but steady voice gave his assessment, even the most brave of the tribal warriors hesitated at the jungle's edge, mouthing the words and nervously studying the rain forest. This was more than they had imagined, more than the mark of a beast.

Of the two American Special Forces advisers who had come running to help—a young sergeant E-5 and a veteran master sergeant—it was the older soldier who understood the weight of what the shaman had said. You might not believe what they believed in, but you had to believe that they believed and that they would react accordingly.

"What's *Kanam*? A snake or something?" asked the younger sergeant as the master sergeant studied the gruesome drag marks and trail left after the attack.

"An evil spirit," the master sergeant said, without looking up. He didn't have to. He already knew what the young sergeant was thinking, which was that there is no such thing as "evil spirits."

Before living in Vietnam, the master sergeant used to think that way, too. Now he wasn't so certain. There were deep, desperate marks; a trail of small troughs really, plowed and clawed into the stream bank where the woman had tried to grab something, anything, to pull herself free, which told him she was still alive as she was being dragged away into the indifferent jungle. A foot on, and the thick venous blood told him her struggle was over. An artery more than likely, maybe the carotid or femoral artery. Small bits of flesh had been scattered in the escape, too; the distinctive and unmistakable prints of a large cat, an Asian tiger, were evident.

"*Kanam*'s their devil, and this sure as hell qualifies. In this case, it's a tiger," he said, turning back to the younger sergeant. "Come on. We're going back to the compound."

"Shouldn't we follow the blood trail and go after the woman? She may still be alive!"

The master sergeant shook his head no. "She's not alive, and we can't really go after the big cat with these," he said, patting his M-16. "We shoot a five-hundred- to six-hundred-pound tiger with a .223 and we'll just piss it off. No, we'll get the shotguns, some heavy slugs, and then go after it. The slugs will bring down a Buick!" Shotguns weren't on the army's approved weapons list, but they were on the shortlist for those who worked the thick rain forests. A shotgun's buckshot rounds could pepper a broad target area; the thumb-size slug rounds could stop a charging tiger.

"What about the woman?"

"She's dead or soon will be. See the dark blood here?" he said, pointing to the maroon spills on the edge of the forest. "That's from a major artery. She struggled for a while and fought back, too, but it ended here."

The younger sergeant's throat went suddenly dry. "Will they come with us?" he asked, staring at the crowd of montagnards who had gathered around the shaman and listened intently to what he had to say.

The master sergeant shrugged. "Her family might. But this is bad business to the rest of them. It's some heavy spiritual shit."

The younger sergeant shook his head and spit. "I don't get it. A tiger eats one of their women, and they blame it on the bogeyman?"

The master sergeant smiled. "You believe in the devil, don't you?" he asked the soldier, whose face registered confusion.

"What kind of question is that?" said the young man.

"Okay, then let's put it another way," said the senior NCO. "You believe in God, right?"

"Of course I do!"

"God and the devil. One usually goes with the other," the master sergeant said, without sarcasm. "Christian missionaries have been trying to convert these people for decades, teaching them about God and the Holy Spirit, not to mention Satan and eternal damnation, too. The trouble is, the montagnards already understand good and evil spirits. In fact, they probably even get a hoot out of some of the biblical stories and appreciate the notion of a vengeful God smiting the crap out of their enemies. However, I don't imagine it's an easy sell, trying to scare them with Satan, especially when their hell is a little closer to earth. They've been at war forever with someone or another; they struggle with monsoons, snakebites, malaria, bad crops, mortar attacks, a shitload of deadly diseases, and even tiger attacks. They catch glimpses of hell on a daily basis."

The young sergeant didn't say anything, not certain how to respond let alone argue the point.

The master sergeant wanted to tell him in combat you can find religion, lose religion or, if you are very lucky, cling to whatever beliefs you held. Instead he tried a different tack. "So, do you believe in luck?"

"Fuck no! There's no such thing as luck."

The master sergeant turned back toward the compound and smiled. "Ah, but you will," he said to himself. "Give you time in this place and you sure as hell will."

When it came time to track the tiger, to make up for his newness, the younger sergeant took the point. The small hunting party cautiously followed his lead. In the dense foliage of the jungle, tracking a man-eater wasn't something you hurried.

The husband and the brother of the dead woman joined the two Americans, but the other warriors in the village did not. The shaman had called for the sacrifice of a water buffalo to appease *Kanam*, and the villagers were busy with the necessary preparations because it was useless trying to track an evil spirit when it could find you anytime it wanted.

The hunting party began at the edge of the rain forest where the blood trail had all but disappeared. Still, there were occasional blood spots, broken twigs, branches, and the large animal's prints that provided a trail. The young NCO moved slowly and carefully in a cloverleaf pattern, covering the immediate area before moving farther into the rain forest. He had never hunted a tiger before but figured it probably wasn't much different from hunting mountain lion. It was a bigger cat, but similar. Of course, back home, he had hunting dogs to tree the big cat. The dogs would hold the scent, track the cougar, and distract it while he would move in and set up his shot.

"Yep, dogs would certainly be nice about now," he said to himself, squeezing the stock of the shotgun. Macho was okay at times; at others it was just plain stupid. Painful, too.

Forty yards on, he raised a hand and held up the others. "Got the body!" he yelled. As the master sergeant eased forward, his eyes darted from the jungle to the tree limbs and tops and back again. The two montagnards covered him as he moved. The scowl on the older NCO's face was sheer frustration.

The young sergeant had yelled because he was afraid, even if he didn't want to admit it. Hell, we all are, the veteran thought, but you don't start yelling when you have just four men in the jungle, even so close to the village and compound. After all, there was still the little matter of the war to consider.

"No sign of the tiger," the young sergeant said as the master sergeant came up beside him. The musky smell of the jungle was giving way to the rancid offal of the corpse. In the high heat of the day, decomposition came swiftly.

"Yeah, well how about the Viet Cong?"

"What?"

"The VC are out here, too, so keep it down," the master sergeant said quietly. He was studying what was left of the corpse. The woman's neck and shoulder were almost severed, and she was missing a large chunk of her left buttock. There were numerous claw marks in her arms and sides where the tiger had slashed at her. Where her left arm had broken backward and dangled, pieces of muscle and flesh hung like red and blue ribbons. Flies flew in erratic patterns over the body or probed the wounds, but what the master sergeant focused on was the fly that was walking across her opened, unblinking eye.

"We can track him," said the young sergeant, confident in his skills and certain that the tiger had not just simply vanished.

"You think so?" The veteran was not sure he wanted to continue after the big cat. There wasn't much of a trail to follow, and the thought of the fly walking across the dead woman's eye left him feeling more than a little uncomfortable. The young sergeant was still new to the war, so he hadn't yet learned to be afraid, or maybe he was just masking it well. To him, it was still a matter of dark curiosity.

The young sergeant nodded and started out. He was hunting and patrolling at the same time. "Hold up!" the master sergeant said. The point man turned around questioningly. "They'll want to take her body back to the village. They'll need help. Hell, we need help," he said.

The master sergeant was right, and the young sergeant knew it. "Besides," added the master sergeant, "the tiger's not going far. Not for a while. He'll be around—especially since he found an easy and reliable source for food."

"The village?"

"Uh-huh. He'll be back, and he'll be hunting us."

"Maybe we can go after it later?"

The senior NCO had another idea. "Better yet. Maybe we can set up a Judas goat and bring him to us."

"A what?"

"A Judas goat, bait for a trap. We stake out a goat or pig or something and sit in a blind and wait until the tiger comes back to eat the bait, which he will."

"And we bag him."

The master sergeant nodded. "And we bag him."

"How about a tree blind? I can set one up in the trees, carry up a 60, wait until he comes for the bait, and then blow him away?" Fired in controlled bursts, an M-60 machine gun was capable of reliably firing hundreds of 7.62mm rounds a minute. The trouble was, you could fire only what you could carry, and if you fired too many rounds through the barrel too quickly, it would begin to melt. Still, in controlled bursts, it was an effective weapon, preferable to a shotgun in a thick jungle, where a burst would fire more rounds across a larger area.

"A tree blind, huh?" The master sergeant thought that had possibilities. A tree blind offered a certain amount of safety a ground position could not.

"Yeah, I can jury-rig a hammock too . . ."

"And tie in a safety line for you, the machine gun, and a radio."

The young sergeant nodded. The idea was sounding better and better. "I'd definitely have the advantage over anything or anyone who came sneaking up on the bait." The plan made more sense than trying to play "great white hunter" on the ground. Tigers ate people. Deer didn't, nor did the moose he had hunted back home. The mountain lion was a challenge. If you weren't armed when you encountered one, you looked at it, raised your hands, and made noise. But you couldn't turn your back on a cougar since the big cat would attack. He figured it probably wasn't much different with tigers, either, except that they could pounce on you and, with a swipe of the claw, splay you open.

Prior to Vietnam, the worst thing he had faced in the woods was a moose. It didn't matter if you faced one of those or not; if you didn't get off a good, well-aimed shot, then it would get mad, charge through underbrush, and stomp the crap out of you. Of course, a moose wouldn't try to cut and slice you like a Veg-O-Matic or think about snacking on you afterward!

"A tree blind might just do it," said the master sergeant.

"Makes sense," the young sergeant said, secretly relieved. "I'll man it!" he added, getting into the plan and showing the veteran NCO he wasn't afraid. "Just give me a 60, and I'll bag the son of a bitch! *Kanam* or no *Kanam!*"

Bravado, thought the master sergeant; the kid wanted to prove he had the stones to do it. The area had been quiet of Communist activity since the younger sergeant arrived in country one month earlier. There had been no recent probes or attacks. Nothing of consequence. The fact that other montagnard tribes were working with the Viet Cong and North Vietnamese may have had something to do with it. Family ties were often stronger than political ties.

Rightly or wrongly, the young sergeant assumed that until he had proved himself in combat, no combat vet would respect him, which was true to some extent. Going after the killer cat might just change all that. It sure as hell would carry some weight with the montagnards, and even the master sergeant couldn't dispute that such a feat would carry a certain cachet. And bagging a tiger would make for one hell of a story.

"I'll talk it over with the Old Man to see what he says," the master sergeant said.

The Old Man was away, leaving the XO—executive officer—in charge. The XO was a young first lieutenant who didn't have a problem with the plan, especially with the tree blind, because it wouldn't be that much different from the listening posts they already used. "How long do we man it?" asked the young officer.

"A few days, three should do it," replied the senior NCO. "I'll monitor the radio."

"Good enough," said the officer. "Good hunting!"

The master sergeant figured he could buy a montagnard's pig that was on its last legs to use as the bait. He'd check out the blind to make sure it had good cover and concealment as well as height. Cats climbed trees, so he figured tigers might be able to climb as well. He'd never seen a picture of one perched on a limb or of a fire department trying to get one down from a tree, but he figured the higher the blind the better.

The plan was good to go. The Judas goat turned out to be a raggedy-ass, old pot-bellied pig that seemed to be aware of its role in the little drama. He didn't go quietly, but then maybe it was the chain collar and leash that he objected to.

When they found a tree that was adequate for the job, one near the stream where the woman had been attacked, they staked the pig to a post near the base of the tree. There was just enough chain to define a radius that would make for an easy target.

With a little help, the young sergeant climbed the tree

and worked his way up through the branches until he found several high up that would support him. With a machete, he began hacking and cutting away any limbs or foliage that might hinder his line of fire.

Once done, he hauled up several empty ammunition boxes and tied them between several sturdy limbs. One would serve as a base for the blind while the second would offer a shelf for the radio and other necessities.

There was no room to sling the hammock he had brought with him, so he tied it to several branches and used it as a seat instead. It would beat sitting on the hard limbs or the ammo box all night.

He tied a poncho above him to shield him from rain or morning dew; the olive drab, waterproof, sheetlike poncho would offer protection from the sun as well. Inside the ammo box, he placed his canteen, a box of C rations, and several grenades. Using an old extraction rope, he pulled up the M-60 light machine gun, a hundred-round belt to lock and load, and an extra hundred that he placed in the second ammo box, just in case. He tied down the 60 and set it between limbs on the base of his blind.

Next, he pulled up a radio that was still attached to the shoulder frame, which made it easier to secure to the tree as it sat in the ammo box. Once he was satisfied with a commo check on the radio, he gave the master sergeant on the ground a thumbs-up. All was right in his world.

The young sergeant had also jury-rigged a pulley system using snap links and rappelling rope, a system that would allow him to exit the thirty-foot-high perch quickly if he had to. All in all, the veteran NCO was impressed.

With little to do but wait, he began camouflaging his blind by pulling in leaves and small branches to hide the platform. It wasn't much of a tree house, but it would do for a night or two. He seriously doubted that even the Viet Cong would notice the blind from the ground.

"You got everything tied down or braced?"

The young sergeant said he did. "Nothing will fall in a sudden wind or something."

"Or something," echoed the master sergeant, leaving it at that.

The master sergeant decided that the platform was high enough in the tree to offer the young sergeant a reasonable amount of protection, even on an outside chance that the tiger would somehow try to climb that high to eat the new guy.

"Looks good," he said, inspecting the blind and testing the rope. "Once you pull up the rope you'll be set to go. I'll bring you out another poncho in case it rains. Other than that, I'd say you've got an outstanding blind." There were broken clouds at the time, but the weather could change quickly. Rain could easily make a long night even longer.

The young sergeant nodded and studied the sky. The master sergeant went back to the camp, retrieved the extra poncho, and returned. Prior to sunset, the master sergeant led the montagnards back to the camp. The husband of the woman who had been killed had been the last to leave.

Night came soon to the jungle. The pinks and purples of sunset gave way to dense black, and the jungle disappeared around him.

To his surprise and delight, there weren't many mosquitoes. At times, he caught himself dozing off, only to be startled awake by the whisper of the wind through the trees.

Once during the night, the pig grunted and startled him awake, again only to teach him a valuable lesson.

When he grabbed the machine gun and tried to maneuver it around the limbs and blind, he hit the limbs and found out that his field of fire was limited. When things settled down again, he had a better idea about what weapon to use in the hunt.

After first light, he called in a negative report, adding that he wanted to return to the camp to make a few changes. When he got the approval, he lowered the rope and then lowered the M-60 machine gun to the ground, hurrying after it. A weapon was useful only if you had it in your hands. On the ground, he slung the machine gun over his shoulder, released the pig, and walked it back into the camp. There he traded in the machine gun for a smaller weapon he could better wield from the perch. He settled on an M-3 grease gun. The short, squat World War II–era tanker's submachine gun was heavy, but the small barrel made it workable in the tree, and the thirty-round clip of .45-caliber rounds, he figured, would definitely do the trick.

An M-16 made every soldier feel like John Wayne. You could hold it in one hand and quickly fire off twenty .223 rounds, quickly reload, and fire all over again. The trouble was, the .223 was basically a high-powered .22, while the .45-caliber bullet of the M-3 had heft and clout; the kind that could take down a '56 Buick or even a tiger. He loaded two magazines, stuffed one in the magazine well and the second one in the right cargo pocket of his jungle fatigues. Sixty rounds and two grenades would be enough.

Going back out to his blind, he chained the pig in place and climbed back up to his perch. He brought along a few more boxes of C rations and a canteen filled with Kool-Aid.

The day proved just as uneventful. He had called in a few commo checks to make sure the radio was working, but other than that, there was nothing much to report. The master sergeant had been helpful with the second poncho, because even though it hadn't rained that morning, the dew was heavy, and the dampness made for bone-numbing cold. However, by early morning, the sun overpowered the jungle, and the usually unbearable heat was surprisingly comfortable in the high perch. A nice breeze blew through the trees.

Sitting in a tree all night and the next day didn't do much for his comfort or disposition, so he modified his seat until he reached a reasonable compromise with the tree. He could stretch out without worrying about falling.

The master sergeant provided him with a pair of binoculars for the second night, reminding the younger soldier they could help him see 20 percent better in the dark.

"The trail winds along the stream bank, and the binoculars should give you a good heads-up if anyone decides to make an unannounced call. Charlie likes predawn visits, too," he said, bringing the young sergeant's attention back to the war. "You see any enemy patrol, you call it in and stay still. No John Wayne shit. You hear me?"

"Uh-huh," said the young sergeant, adding, "Thanks" for the binoculars.

"No problem."

Night two came. From his roost, an adjustment of the focus on the binoculars brought the village into sharp focus. The montagnards went through their evening activities around the fires much the way their ancestors had for centuries. He shook his head at their naïveté, thinking that their unchanged routines kept them in the Stone Age. He had heard the litany of praises—yada-yada loyal and fierce, yada-yada small people, big hearts. But they lived in crude huts on stilts and kept pigs below their living quarters. They ate monkey brain and dog and relished blood soup, didn't have a written language, believed in evil spirits, and they were subsistence slash-and-burn farmers.

The montagnard men, at times, preferred loincloths to uniforms and small crossbows to rifles. The women wore ankle-length skirts, smoked pipes, and tagged along behind their men carrying baskets as they suckled small children. Every so often, the young sergeant had to look over his shoulder to make sure *National Geographic* wasn't behind him with a camera, filming it all and saying, "Cover shot! Cover shot!"

"*Kanam*, my ass!" he said, turning away from the village and turning the binoculars into the black abyss that was the rain forest. In the dim light, he could make out a few limbs and foliage but not much more. Everything else was lost in a maze of black and gray shadow. The cicadas and their insect noises and an occasional lonely cry from an unseen bird reassured him all was otherwise quiet along his western front.

The first night, the pig protested with grunts and groans at the discomfort of being tied to a stake with the heavy chain. But by the second night, it had settled down, sleeping soundly against the base of the tree. The young sergeant had named it "Bait" and thought of the pig with fondness, especially since the pig was an effective early warning system for anything that disturbed or threatened them. Early on the second morning, in the hour prior to dawn, Bait began to squeal and grunt nervously. The young sergeant came awake with a start and stared down into the blackness, his heart pounding in his chest. He grabbed the binoculars and saw nothing, so he set them down and brought up the grease gun, aiming it at the jungle floor below. He listened closely for the noise he was certain a tiger would make. Six-hundred-pound tigers had to make *some* noise, especially in dense underbrush. But he heard nothing except grunts and squeals from the pig.

Something in the rain forest frightened him; something that was too close for Bait's comfort. In a jungle, that could mean any number of things, few of them pleasant.

The local vegetation was very thick, so he expected to hear the sounds of breaking when it was pushed aside. But there was just the hushed scraping of something slithering across the rain-forest floor, and then the *plop* from the stream a few seconds later. Snake, the young sergeant said to himself, laughing quietly at his own nervousness as he fought to steady his breathing and his nerves.

At sunrise, he studied the surrounding jungle, decided it was safe, and then lowered the radio from the perch and hurriedly followed. Bait was up and at his feet as he freed the pig from the chain at the base of the tree and then walked him back to camp. What could be finer than a man walking his pig?

After securing his weapon and tying Bait to a post outside the TOC, he gave his report and then left with his charge to find something to eat. Later, they slept, he in his cot and the thin pig at the door of the bunker, lying in the warm dirt of the Vietnamese day with no thought of the previous evening's chore and the new evening's mission. It was all becoming routine.

The third night was dark. A cloud mass covered most of the early-evening sky, and what little moonlight there was barely filtered through the foliage. There was a threat of rain, and the slight wind carried a dampness and chill that disturbed the NCO. Rain would only complicate matters. Below, he could just make out Bait, who was nestled in the crook of a large root that spread several feet from the base of the tree and harbored him from the wind. The pig was only a gray shadow against a black backdrop.

Just as he had the evening before, the young sergeant spent the first hour of his hunt studying the village before turning his attention back to the jungle. He huddled beneath his rubber-lined poncho, watching and listening to the rain forest, and he wasn't certain when he slipped into a light sleep. He was certain that it was the squeals of the pig that brought him instantly awake. The thin pig was stumbling over the chain as he desperately tried to chew through the links. This time, though, the NCO didn't hear anything slither or plop. There was just the sound of branches brushing one another in the breeze.

The grease gun didn't have a safety, just a hinge that fit over the large thick bolt and kept it from firing. The grease gun was a spring-operated, fixed-bolt weapon that worked on concussion. When the trigger released the tension from the springs and the thick fixed bolt slammed forward, firing the chambered round, the concussion sent the bolt back for the next round, and so on until the magazine was empty.

The young soldier thumbed the hinge open and reached in and pulled the bolt back, cocking the weapon as he tried to focus on the scene below. The metallic click of the bolt locking back resounded through the jungle and the young sergeant swore at his own foolishness. At least no one else was around to hear it, or so he hoped.

The pig was still squealing, and the anguished sound sent a shiver through the young sergeant's body. He had expected to hear the growls or deep guttural rip of a tiger or what he thought a tiger should sound like. But he heard only the pig's frightened squeals.

A slight breeze pushed across the stream and rustled

the underbrush, a faint scraping sound that faded with the momentary gust of wind. Was someone or something down there?

The young sergeant strained to find the cause of the scraping sound, figuring it had to be another snake, which didn't make him feel any less easy. Then he remembered that snakes could slither up trees! He immediately turned his gaze to the tree limbs around him so he never heard the tiger's leap. Only the woeful din of the pig's slaughter and a god-awful cry from the big cat caused him to turn his attention back to the ground, where a large shadow overpowered the pig, instantly silencing it. For a long moment, he was transfixed by the scene below as the deadly swirl of shadows ended the pig's struggle. Within seconds, the tiger had pounced on the pig, killing it only after realizing the chain wouldn't allow it to be carried away.

The young sergeant's hands were shaking as he quickly aimed at the shadow below and fired abrupt bursts from the thirty-round clip.

The tiger half twisted and snarled upward as it was hit, recognizing a threat. But it didn't fall or lie down and die. Instead, it stumbled back over the exposed roots, turning back on the tree, and clawing and slashing at its base. The big cat hissed and growled, striking out repeatedly at both the tree and the carcass of the dead pig.

The young sergeant didn't have a clear shot, but he fired again anyway, and the tiger's cry was unnerving as it leaped away, crashing through the underbrush. The sergeant followed the sound of its passage with another burst from the grease gun. He had only two magazines, and one was almost empty. His palms were wet, and adrenaline was pumping through him.

The radio was alive with calls from the compound,

calling for a situation report. The young sergeant ignored it and kept his eyes locked on the darkened kill zone. Bait wasn't moving or making a sound. When he was certain it was safe, he picked up the radio's handset.

"Safari. This is Zoo Master. What's going on? Over."

"It was the tiger!" he said into the radio's handset. The master sergeant on the other end asked if he had killed it.

"Negative," he replied, hesitantly. He realized how scared he probably sounded. He took a deep breath. "It ran off into the jungle. I say again, it ran off into the jungle." Just as he said that, the wounded tiger returned to the tree from a new direction, his growl more animated, his anger more feral and primordial.

Then the wounded tiger jumped toward his roost, clawing at the limbs below before falling back hard against the ground. He still hadn't had a good look at the creature and saw it only in a series of frightening glimpses, but what he had seen scared the shit out of him.

"Fuck!" the young sergeant cried, reeling back in his harness and scrambling to let off another burst. This time, though, he knew he was off target. Then the bolt locked back, telling him the first magazine was empty. He heard the wounded tiger sniffing at him below, and as he grabbed for the second magazine, he fumbled and dropped it, then almost fell himself, trying to catch it as it rebounded off the side of the tree and careened into the underbrush.

"Oh fuck!" he said. "Fuck! Fuck! Fuck!"

"Safari. This is Zoo Master. Do you need assistance?" The young sergeant wasn't about to tell him or the others he'd lost his ammunition. The wounded tiger was pacing the stream bank, seemingly unconcerned with the tree or the annoyance in it. But when a branch snapped back against its wound, the tiger struck out and roared. Then, when it realized there was no threat, the big cat paced again. The young sergeant reached for a grenade.

The radio call took his immediate attention off the big cat. "I say again, do you need assistance?"

"Negative," the young sergeant said, holding on to the grenade while trying to pick his next course of action from a host of options—none of which involved getting down from the tree. "It's okay. He ran off. I'll continue to monitor."

"You sure?"

"Roger," lied the young sergeant as he wondered if he was high enough in the tree and whether he could climb even higher. His mouth was dry again, and he felt fear turn his intestines into something churning and liquid. He still couldn't see the tiger. All he could really make out was the violent noise and ominous mix of shadows. Then there was nothing, which unnerved him more. Was the tiger still down there or had he taken off?

He was rattled and didn't sleep the rest of the night.

At first light, after carefully scouring the forest floor and the stream bank beyond, he pulled himself up to a standing position to lower himself out of the tree. Nothing moved below as he shifted on the limbs and turned to climb down.

All the while, he was craning to get a better look, peering over and around the tree's limbs and listening to every sound and nuance of the early morning. Birds were chirping, but what did that mean anyway? "Eat the soldier when he climbs down from the tree?"

Life was tough, but tougher yet—and brief—if you were stupid. Lowering himself in stages, he kept his eyes on the jungle. When he was reasonably satisfied the tiger wasn't present, he hurriedly lowered himself.

Once on the ground, he was out of the harness in an

instant, scurrying to find the second magazine, locking and loading it into the magazine well, ready to fire at any damn thing that moved. He was relieved to have the magazine in the gun for several reasons. The first and most immediate was the wounded tiger, while the second had to do with it being found out that the great white hunter had lost half his ammunition.

Tiger hunting was nothing like hunting cougar at all, he was beginning to think, and a frightening understanding slowly closed in around him. It was the realization that he was a good shot and had fired thirty rounds at the animal but only wounded it. He sure as shit hadn't killed it, since it came back at him and almost had managed to scale the tree. His hands were moist and wet as he studied the deep lacerations its claws had left in the bark, shredded fifteen feet up. For the most part, he had been relatively safe. But at night, in the dark, when the wounded tiger leaped, the young soldier's imagination closed the gap.

The morning sky was a mass of tumbling gray-and-black clouds as a storm was moving in over the region. Soon it would rain, and any trail the animal left would be washed away.

There was no sign of the tiger other than occasional splotches of blood that could as easily have come from Bait. The thin pig was torn in two, and the half that included the head had been carried off. Left behind was one big bloody ham and some entrails.

In the distance, he saw the master sergeant leading a small group of montagnards out to assess the results of the blind hunt. The montagnards spread out on line and had their rifles pointed ahead of them as they moved. They were not about to be surprised. By the time they had worked their way to him, thunder boomed in the distance.

"You okay?" asked the master sergeant, studying what was left of the dead pig and the mess on the jungle floor.

The younger sergeant shrugged. "I think I wounded it, but in the dark, I probably shot more brush than anything else. It got away."

"Yeah, well maybe it crawled away to die. Maybe not," said the master sergeant as his eyes traversed the immediate area.

"Jesus, I wish I would've bagged the son of a bitch."

"Yeah, well, wounding it is a good start. Go on and collect your stuff, and we'll head back to camp before it rains."

The young sergeant nodded and handed the grease gun to the senior NCO. The truth of it was that he wasn't all that thrilled about taking the fight to the tiger anyway.

Behind him a sudden cold gust of wind rustled in the underbrush, and the young sergeant turned back in fear to face the attack that never came. A single droplet of cold sweat trickled down his back, sending a chill through him that resonated to his core.

The master sergeant saw the younger man's reaction and turned as well. It's nothing at all, nothing but *Kanam*, he thought.

THE *NGUOI RUNG*

We're all familiar with stories of Big Foot and Sasquatch sightings and even the tales of the Yeti of the snow-covered mountains of Tibet. Now it's time to introduce you to the Vietnamese version of Big Foot.

They were taking a breather. The six-man patrol from the 101st Airborne Division's LRRPs was set up in a protective wagon-wheel position—heads facing outward, feet pointed toward the center—as secure a formation as the terrain would allow. And it wasn't allowing much.

The behind-the-lines patrol had taken them into a remote and difficult stretch of mountainous jungle in the Central Highlands. The terrain was rugged and steep, and at night, the LRRPs had to wedge themselves between trees to keep from slipping or sliding downhill.

Wiping the sweat from their eyes and leaning against their heavy rucksacks, the tired LRRPs tended to loosen straps or realign equipment as they rested—all the while watching and listening to the jungle around them.

On quiet guard, the six soldiers were facing out against the wall of green-and-brown underbrush, guarding against any Viet Cong who might have tracked them or who might happen upon them by chance.

The combined weight of their rucksacks, weapons,

and LBE—the load-bearing-equipment harness that held their web gear—was one hundred pounds or so, and climbing the steep hills with that kind of load took some doing. So the break was a momentary but necessary respite.

Gary Linderer was thinking that the surrounding jungle was quiet and deceptively peaceful. The forest noises—the occasional rustling of the wind through the trees, the grunts of an animal in the distance, and the sound of birds—could easily lull a soldier into a false sense of serenity even though the war was very much around them. However, if anything was out of the ordinary, there was no indication. That is, until the small trees and underbrush just fifteen yards uphill began to shake violently.

Linderer's attention and the frenzied focus of the other team members turned to the commotion. On guard, the LRRPs brought up their weapons and waited. Linderer was the closest team member to the hubbub, and his heart was jumping in his chest as he watched and waited for the intruder.

While he was ready for a Viet Cong soldier, he wasn't ready for the face that peered through the underbrush. If it was a Viet Cong soldier, then it was a damn ugly one! An oblong head framed the hair-covered face. Dark, deep-set eyes lay beneath a prominent brow, and they did nothing to complement the heavy jowls and angry mouth. As it stepped into a small clearing, Linderer could see that matted reddish-brown hair ran down the creature's neck and covered most of its body. Whatever it was, it stood at least five feet tall, had broad shoulders, long thick muscular arms, and a heavy torso. It walked upright. In the small clearing, it stopped and studied the Americans.

"What the hell is that?" someone called out from behind Linderer.

"It's a rock ape," said another team member. Another team member disagreed. "No, it ain't," he said. "I've seen rock apes, and that sure as hell isn't a rock ape!"

"It's an orangutan, isn't it?" Linderer asked while the others kept their eyes glued on the strange creature.

"Well, if it is, then he can't read a map. There are no orangutans in Vietnam."

The apelike creature soon lost interest in the six LRRPs, turned back the way it had come, and easily climbed back up the steep rise. "It's an ape of some kind," one of the LRRPs said. "It has to be."

But then, maybe it wasn't.

In the Central Highlands region of Vietnam in the remote province of Kontum where the country bumps up against Cambodia and Laos, there is mounting evidence of the existence of strange, humanlike creatures the locals call the *nguoi rung*—"The people of the forest." Big Foot.

While the montagnards and other tribal peoples have believed that the nonhuman species have inhabited the region for centuries, scientists now say there may be something more to the folktale and legend.

Toward the end of the American war in Vietnam, numerous sightings by Viet Cong and NVA soldiers of apelike creatures walking upright became so overwhelming that the North Vietnamese party secretariat ordered scientists into the region to investigate the *nguoi rung* while the war was still going on.

In 1974, as the North Vietnamese Army and the Viet Cong pushed south to overrun the country, Professor Vo Quy of the Vietnam national university was sent into the region to conduct an investigation. Vo Quy discovered a *nguoi rung* footprint on the forest floor and made a cast of the impression, which was analyzed and studied by Vietnamese academics. It was wider than a human footprint and too big for an ape. The unusual find added credence to the folktale. It also set off debate in the scientific arena. Other expeditions were mounted but yielded few results. Chance sightings of the *nguoi rung* continued, ranging from small creatures to larger ones. Eyewitnesses had differences of opinion as to the exact color of the creatures' body hair. Like those sighted earlier, these latest *nguoi rung* walked upright and were described as having human characteristics.

In 1982, Professor Tran Hong Viet became the second scientist to discover *nguoi rung* footprints, and while scientists debated the actual existence of such creatures, many of the critics' arguments went up in smoke when zoologist John MacKinnon and a team of scientists discovered three previously unknown mammals in the Vu Quang Mountain rain forest in 1992.

The discovery of the new mammals demonstrated that the remote regions might well hold other new discoveries, including clues that might solve the riddle of Vietnam's Bigfoot.

Ironically, it was MacKinnon who, in 1969, came across manlike footprints in the jungles of Borneo, ascribed by locals to the *Batutat*, i.e., Bigfoot. MacKinnon wrote that "the toes of the creature looked quite human . . ." and that the tracks would have been about the right size for the Asiatic black bear. However, the only bear known in Borneo is the sun bear, which is considerably smaller.

To this day, the controversy continues even as international teams of scientists scour the remote mountain jungles looking for what the local villagers say has always been there.

REMEMBER TO DIE

It was General Douglas MacArthur, quoting an old song, who said "Old Soldiers never die, they just fade away." But what if they linger and refuse to go? What if they forget to die? Here's one veteran's story of his unusual encounter with an old soldier.

For the dead are not powerless, did I say? There is no death, only a change of worlds.

—CHIEF SEALTH

Today he is a quiet, deeply religious, dark-suit conservative who just happens to be a Vietnam veteran. In 1967, uncertain of his direction or convictions, he had dropped out of college "to find himself." His draft board found him first and soon afterward changed his 2-A student status to that of 1-A "draftable," which is exactly what happened less than a few months later when he received a telegram that began, "Greetings from the President of the United States." The president didn't know him from Adam, but his draft board did and sent him for an induction physical in Seattle. That same day, he was bused to nearby Fort Lewis, where he underwent basic and advanced infantry training with thousands of other draftees.

After sixteen weeks or so of learning how to survive jungle combat in the cold rain and snow of Washington, he declined an offer to attend Jump School or the twelve-week NCO course. So he received orders for Vietnam. First, though, he enjoyed an all too fast thirty-day leave before reporting to the overseas processing center at the south end of the fort. There he was issued temporary bedding, was told to find a bunk in any of the center's old World War II barracks, was issued jungle fatigues, and spent a lackluster three days waiting for his name to be called for a flight to Vietnam. When it came during an afternoon formation, he turned in his bedding, clambered aboard one of a number of buses with his duffel bag and orders, along with the other hundred or so G.I.'s who were making the trip, and was driven to nearby McChord Air Force Base.

From McChord, it was a short flight to Alaska, a longer flight to Japan, and then another uncomfortable leg to Vietnam. At the replacement center, he was assigned to the 1st Cavalry Division, the "Cav," where he served as an infantryman, a grunt, during his tour of duty.

When he returned home, he used his G.I. Bill to finish college, which is where he met his wife. He has been married to the same woman for over twenty years, owns a fashionably comfortable home with a reasonable mortgage, has kids who actually like him, and has had a successful career in financial management. He does well.

Since we're friends, and knowing that I write humorous as well as off-the-wall stories for *Behind the Lines* magazine, he admitted that he had something that might be of interest to me.

"Like what? Your canteen run out of Perrier during your tour of duty, you being a yuppie and all?"

"Naw. I hired my own water bearer," he said. "You were one of those cowboys with the 1st of the 9th, as I recall."

"Yes, Your Grace. But *we* didn't drink water; we only drank good whiskey, like all real Cav men did and do." Since I didn't have a beer can to bend and knew that he couldn't see me scratch myself or snort, I chuckled instead.

"So how unusual is your story? Good unusual, mediocre unusual, or ho-hum 'oh no, grandpa's telling his war stories again' unusual?" I asked.

"I'm not a grandfather yet, and the story's good enough for you to buy me a halfway decent imported beer as you listen in awe."

"Awe, huh?"

"Uh-huh. That's your typical dumbfounded expression," he said, getting even for the Perrier and grandpa remark. "Actually, it isn't all that much of a story, but it's a great excuse to get together to be 'guys' and drink beer."

The trouble with successful business types is that they don't have bowling leagues. I suggested we get together on a Tuesday evening around seven at a place called Pegasus Pizza on Alki Beach in West Seattle. I told him Pegasus makes great Greek-style pizza and fresh shrimp salads that nobody does better, and I said that if his story was a bust, then at least the food wouldn't be.

"You bring your 'good enough' story, and I'll bring my notebook and awe."

To beat the early dinner crowd, we agreed on the following Tuesday just after work. A steady rain began to fall as I rounded Alki Beach, and like most other spring days in Seattle, a steady rain was part of the scenario. In spite of his song, I was certain that Perry Como probably had never lived in Seattle or, perhaps if he had, he would have understood that the "bluest skies he had ever seen" were just then hiding behind at least two more months of gray skies. In the light rain, a green-and-white ferry on its way to Bainbridge Island was skating across Puget Sound, sending waves in its wake that rolled over the broad flat beach where Seattle actually began. In the late 1800s, the settlers called it "Seattle Alki," which to the locals then meant "New York by and by." When the Big Apple failed to bob, the pioneers rowed across Elliott Bay and settled on the hillside that became the actual city. Rain runs better downhill.

I found a place to park just up from the restaurant and, dodging die-hard joggers and bicyclists who confused the sidewalk for the Tour de France course, I raced inside. Since it was early, I got a table near the window, ordered a pitcher of a local microbrew and two glasses. Even with the rain, Puget Sound offers a good view, better behind glass while holding one. My yuppie grunt friend arrived a few minutes later as the waitress brought over the beer.

"You know what they call two days of sunshine in a row in Seattle?" he said, shrugging out of a fashionable Gore-Tex parka.

"Yeah. Summer," I said while he placed the parka on an empty seat.

"The rain is depressing," he said.

"Which is why God gave us beer." I poured, tilting the glass to minimize the foam. My well-practiced technique didn't seem to impress him. "So tell me why you think your story deserves beer and pizza."

"Yeah, well it probably doesn't," he admitted. "In fact, the more I think about it, the more I think it probably wasn't real," he said with an embarrassed shrug.

"Oh sure. Now you tell me!" I said, feigning distress.

"For bullshit war stories, I usually order light beer. We're talking a pitcher of good microbrew here, buddy boy."

He laughed, but drank his beer anyway. "I'll tell you what. I'll buy," he said.

I shook my head. "Naw! My treat. Besides, if the story really is weak, I'll just water down your beer some."

"So, why are we friends again?"

"I dunno, you have low standards?"

He laughed again, loosening up. "Must be," he said. "Anyway, I don't even know why I'm telling you this except that I thought it's your kind of story."

"Strange, you mean?"

He nodded. "Do you write any other kind?"

"Yeah, well . . ." I said as I opened my notebook and flipped through a few pages of the chicken scratches that are my handwriting. It was better than shorthand because no one else could read it; even I sometimes had to go over it a few times before I finally recognized what it said. Secrets really were secret. I turned a few more pages, and when I found a few blanks, I was ready. "Okay, let's hear it," I said as he sat back and laughed.

"This isn't your standard war story," he said. "I mean, it's not the typical 'There I was with the shoeshine kid who had a booby-trapped grenade' kind or, say, the barber from the base barbershop who turns out to be a Viet Cong colonel found dead in the wire after an attack on the camp. No, this one is different," he added, and then laid out terms. "This has gotta be worth a fairly decent pizza. How's their house special?"

"Great, but tell me the war story first. Then we'll barter over who's paying for the toppings."

My friend laughed and leaned closer in his conspiracy. "Okay, sport. Here it is. We were on a platoon recon just outside of Phan Thiet . . ."

"Phan Thiet is on the coast, isn't it?"

The storyteller nodded. "Yep, right on the South China Sea. It's still in II Corps, but south, damn near to Vung Tau." He slowed down to let me write, and then charged back into his war story when I was ready.

Although I wasn't quite certain where Phan Thiet was, I smiled, remembering the coastal town of Vung Tau that the French had called Cap Saint-Jacques. The white sand beaches of the resort town were a great in-country R & R site for G.I.'s and, some said, even for the Viet Cong. Maybe so. It was quiet and tranquil enough to make the war seem remote and distant.

"When were you in Phan Thiet?"

"Early '68. And this happened a month or so after Tet. There was still a lot of Viet Cong activity, and our job was to ambush any units that were moving south, on Saigon. Anyway, on our tenth day out, in a small valley, we found a well-used trail along a stream, so the company commander had our platoon monitor it.

"While the company spread out along a jungle mountain hillside, our platoon was set up for the night on a ridge overlooking the trail. Our job was to ambush any Viet Cong who decided to walk down the trail. Any of the VC who hadn't been caught in our kill zone would try to flank us and end up walking or running right into the rest of the company.

"We set up just before sunset, dug in, and tried to get comfortable, which wasn't all that easy since it was a cold, foggy night, and the ground was wet, muddy, and miserable.

"I was up just before first light—in fact, I took over a guard shift from four to six in the morning. I did a commo check on the radio, and when I got the response I was expecting, I leaned against my rucksack and made myself as comfortable as I could.

"There were some people who hated this shift, but not me," he said. "I liked it. It was usually quiet and peaceful when the sun came up over the jungle or mountains."

"Not always, though," I added. He agreed.

"No, not always. It was also a time when Charlie sometimes hit with ground probes or attacks, fucking up that first morning cup of coffee."

Predawn attacks were one of the tactics the Viet Cong and NVA employed. Hit the enemy when he least expected it. Still, there were times in the predawn hours when the countryside of Vietnam looked its most serene. It was a dangerous beauty and powerfully seductive.

My grunt friend went on with his story. "Anyway, I checked my rifle and laid it on my lap, made sure the claymore clacker was close at hand, and then settled in to watching the jungle in front of me."

The "claymore clacker" was the triggering device for the claymore antipersonnel mine. The claymore was a shaped-charge antipersonnel mine. It held two pounds of plastic explosive and over seven hundred ball bearings, and when detonated, it devastated anyone and anything in its path.

"I was still a little groggy as I stared out over the valley. But by the light of even a quarter moon, I could tell that there wasn't too much to see. We had good cover, and anyone coming at us would have to climb up to us, and in the twilight or early morning, even a rainy one, it wouldn't be tactically smart. We were in a good position, but being so close to the South China Sea, the morning dew made everything cold and damp."

I laughed. "It's funny how most people think Vietnam was always hot," I said, remembering just how cold it could get in the jungle at night after the sun had set and how, by early morning, just before sunrise, you sometimes had to huddle against your rucksack, poncho liner, and poncho trying to get warm. It was worse when it rained. The word *miserable* comes to mind, as do a few choice swearwords. Looking at the rain falling outside the restaurant, the experience was there again, if only briefly. It wasn't a flashback, just the power of memory.

"Yeah, at night, though, it was another matter," he said, going on with his story, "which is when it happened."

"When what happened?"

"I don't know. I was cold and tired, so it probably was just a dream, maybe . . ."

"What '*maybe*'? So what did you see?" I said, looking up from my notebook. Actually, I was looking for the waitress. Thinking about the cold mornings in Vietnam made the thought of a hot pizza more appealing.

"You'll think it's stupid," he said, frowning.

"Not until you tell me," I said, turning back to face him. "Then I'll think it's stupid, but I promise not to laugh until I get home. I'm a sensitive nineties kind of guy. You weren't smoking dope when you saw your vision, were you?"

"No, I wasn't then. I never actually smoked a lot of dope," he said, nervously. I suspected that maybe his company or clients wouldn't like knowing that someone managing their accounts had done drugs, even the soft ones.

"Never inhaled, you mean?"

"Not if you expect to run for public office or, say, handle people's money. People get nervous when they find out you were once human."

I smiled. I knew some people in sensitive positions who wouldn't or couldn't admit it, either, not if they expected to keep their jobs. I had a few friends in the military who had drinking problems, courtesy of the military. Over years of mandatory and frequent "Hail and Farewells," officer and NCO club functions, and various other social and professional activities where they were encouraged to drink, some became functioning alcoholics. However, in today's military, it is unacceptable to have an alcohol problem, so the career NCOs and officers keep it to themselves and their families.

"How did you handle that question on your job questionnaires?" he asked.

"I said I 'experimented' with drugs in my youth, which to them said it 'explained a great deal.' My only drug of choice for the last twenty years has been caffeine, which adds a whole new meaning to 'scoring some good Colombian'!"

I raised a hand to get the waitress's attention, and she smiled, nodded, and mouthed the words "One minute!"

"So what do you want on your pizza?"

"Anything with extra cheese," he replied.

I nodded, and when the waitress came over to our table, I handed her the menu. The waitress was a young, lithe blonde with warm eyes, which we eventually noticed. "We'll have a large special with extra cheese," I said, while she wrote down the order and smiled again before walking away. We both sighed as we watched her leave.

"Did you notice that she smiled at me?" I said, finally.

"Yeah, well, she probably smiles at her grandfather," my friend said as he refilled our glasses.

"You don't think she thinks we're geezers, do you?"

"She didn't bother to check our IDs for the beer, did she?" he said with an air of authority. "Besides, she's probably adding Geritol to the shredded cheese even as we speak."

We sighed again, both of us realizing that we were from another time and era, and she belonged to the "here and now." Here-and-now people were still young enough to believe the world was their oyster; we were jaded enough to know there were red tides. Turning back to my friend, I said, "Okay, you got the extra cheese. So what happened, and what exactly or almost exactly did you see in the morning mist?"

He picked up his glass, took a long sip, and then set the glass down as he stared out the window overlooking a small copy of the Statue of Liberty on Alki Beach. Although Alki was the birthplace of Seattle, the town itself was named after the Indian chief Sealth who welcomed the settlers and opened the region to them. The Indians didn't have a term for real estate development or "tall single lattes with no foam," so the settlers introduced them by parceling off the property and leaving just enough room for the first Starbucks.

"It wasn't all that misty," he said, turning back from the window. "One minute it's quiet and I'm staring out over the hillside as the sun was coming up, thinking Vietnam would really be a beautiful country if it wasn't for the war. I mean, it's lush, green, and, at times, really pretty."

"Yeah, at times," I echoed. My mind raced back to a jungle stream and small wooden bridge our reconnaissance platoon had found outside of Song Be in 1969. For a moment, I was overwhelmed by the natural beauty and tranquil setting. There were bright purple and yellow wildflowers, lime-green grasses, and thick bamboo stalks in myriad shades of brown and green. Those, combined with the carefully crafted wooden bridge, bright blue sky, and sunshine, made the war briefly disappear.

Briefly. But then, the war always had a way of slamming you back into the real moment, with a fresh enemy footprint leading up to the bridge or worse, with the first rounds of a Viet Cong ambush tearing through the scenic underbrush and coming straight at you.

"Of course, at other times, it was downright scary."

"No kidding. I mean I'm staring at the jungle, but my mind's wandering, and the next thing I know, an old soldier suddenly appears in front of me. I mean, he was right *there*! I was startled, brought my rifle up, and was staring down the sights leveled at his chest. The trouble was, the old guy was hovering over the edge of the ridge, floating in midair. It wasn't real."

I nodded, remembering something similar myself. I was pulling a predawn guard shift in the bush and, like my friend, I was a little groggy, too, and my mind was anywhere but on the war. Coming out of my thoughts, I saw him, an NVA sapper, and he was standing a few yards away crouched and standing perfectly still, hoping I wouldn't notice him. He was maybe all of fifteen yards away, and I knew he was on his way to kill me. Slowly, I eased my hand to the grip of my rifle. Leveled it on my thighs, knowing I couldn't miss him at that range, and waited for him to move, to flinch or anything so I could blow him away. It was cold, and I was trembling, and I probably held the position for what seemed like an eternity until the sun came over the horizon, filtered through the trees, and turned the NVA sapper into a small tree.

"Imagination's a funny thing. It tends to wander when you're tired or, say, stressed, and man were we stressed," he offered, picking up his glass and taking another drink. "We were just too young and dumb to know it at the time."

I nodded again, thinking that although we were too young then to understand about its lasting consequences, we had learned new definitions of the word *fear*. "It took over at times and manipulated everything, even the rational mind," I said, feeling damn near intellectual until some of the beer I was sipping dribbled down my chin and onto my shirt. Intellectual depth only goes so far.

"Fear makes us think and believe a lot of things our eyes tell us can't be true, only we're too frightened not to believe them. You know what I'm saying?"

"Uh-huh, I do."

"There are times since the war when I've been more afraid thinking about some of the things that happened or could have happened than how I was when they happened. I wasn't adequately frightened then."

"Older and wiser," I said, and continued with my intellectual approach. "So the old soldier's just standing there in midair, and he's what, Casper Cong, the friendly fucking VC or NVA ghost?"

"Not at first," he said, staring at his glass. "No, at first I think maybe he's one of our guys taking a piss or something, only it wasn't. He was a soldier all right, only he's something out of a gladiator movie. He's wearing a leather helmet, his right hand was on a short sword in a metal and leather sheath, while he's holding a battered, oblong shield that had seen better times in the other."

I chuckled. "A gladiator, huh? You sure it wasn't Kirk Douglas on a bad Bob Hope tour?"

"Nope. No Kirk Douglas. This guy was dressed in something like long johns, only cut off at the elbows and knees. No elaborate breastplates or anything . . ."

"Jethro meets Spartacus?"

"Complete with cape and sandals, Mr. Clampett."

I had heard a lot of stories, but this one had taken a turn I hadn't expected, and my face must have registered as much. Smirking is expected of me. Quiet thoughtful interest isn't.

"Now you see why I wanted the extra cheese first," he added. "Crazy, huh?"

"I don't know," I said, remembering what had happened to me. "I once saw an enemy soldier turn into a tree."

"Yeah, but I bet he didn't talk to you, did he?"

I shook my head. "No, he didn't. So you and your guy had a meaningful conversation, did you?"

"Not really," he said, ordering another pitcher of beer while giving the waitress his platinum card. "Would you put the pizza and beer on this, please," he said to the young woman, and then back to me said, "It's on me. With your interviewing skills, I can't imagine you're actually making a living at writing, so you listen, and I'll pay."

"If I had pride, I'd be hurt," I said, while he shook his head in protest.

"Naw. My story. My treat. Besides, you're cheaper than therapy." We were temporarily interrupted when the pizza arrived, and we peeled away a few slices from the tray and momentarily planted them on a plate.

"So what did Spartacus say?" I asked, picking up a piece while a long line of mozzarella cheese struggled to hold on to the tray. I broke it off and wrapped it around the slice.

"He said something, only I didn't understand it at the time . . ."

"Like what? All Vietnam is divided into three parts and that Gauls you, right?"

My friend put his slice of pizza on a plate and actually cut it with a knife and fork, while I folded mine in on itself and ate it New York style. Long before he had finished his first slice, I was well into my second.

"You ever wonder why you don't make a living as a full-time writer?"

"No," I said, "not really. So what did he say?" I asked again, taking another bite and wondering what kind of person eats pizza with a knife and fork. Maybe he was crazy after all?

"Meant to Mary," he said, matter of fact.

"Meant to Mary?"

He nodded again but didn't elaborate.

"Okay. I give. What does it mean?"

"Nothing for a long time. To me, anyway," he said. "Actually, it turned out to be Latin."

"You get that from your altar boy days at Our Lady of the Holy Bingo Game? Let me guess, Catholic guilt, right?"

"I'm Methodist," he said, shaking his head. "We don't do guilt. Just potluck dinners and bake sales. Anyway, I had no idea what it meant, which is why I suspected it was a waking dream. The old soldier nods as though I should understand it all, and I nod back, thinking I'm maybe nodding off, and then he disappears in the sunrise coming up over the valley."

"So, that's it?" I said, taking another bite of the slice of pizza.

"Sort of," he said. "That's most of it. The rest is *X-Files* or *Twilight Zone* material . . ."

"How's that? What do you mean?" I said, putting down my pizza and offering what appeared to be my focused attention. Actually, the hot cheese from the pizza was clinging to the roof of my mouth, and my "focused" attention was trying to pull the cheese down and the skin connected to it with my tongue.

"Did you know that the Roman Empire stretched from England to Iran, and its influence went a great deal further, so maybe it's not unlikely they might have made an exploration trip to Vietnam."

"Vespas get good mileage, and they have those plastic little windshields to catch bugs," I said. He ignored me, again.

"The Romans, like the Vikings, got everywhere, or tried to. The spooky thing is when I told a schoolteacher friend of mine the story, she listened like you're doing now, and then when I got to the part about 'Meant to Mary' she shook her head and said I had it wrong."

"No Romans in Vietnam?"

"No. She said that part was possible but not likely. The Greeks found a sea route to China in the first century B.C., and there was even a professor at Oxford University who was convinced that the Romans made it that far."

"To Vietnam?"

He shrugged. "Possibly," he said. "Chinese legends also talk about foreign mercenary soldiers who sacked a Chinese city or two."

"Roman soldiers?"

"Well, foreign mercenary soldiers whose look, weapons, and tactics fit the description. Of course, there are academics who claim it wasn't possible, too."

I thought for a moment, recalling something I had read about Marco Polo and how, after he made it back from China, not too many academics believed some of his account either. I said as much.

"I don't put much stock in experts," I said as he offered another example.

"In the 1800s, nobody believed John Colter either when he described the geysers and bubbling mud at Yellowstone."

"Colter?"

"He was originally part of the Lewis and Clark expedition, but stayed behind to hunt and scout. He and another trapper were captured by the Indians in Montana, and as I recall, the trapper was killed, and Colter was stripped of his clothing, weapons, everything."

"So he lived with the Indians at Yellowstone?"

"No," he said. "They had something else planned for him. After they stripped him, they made him run for it. Then, when he had a hundred-yard or so lead, they sent out warriors one at a time to kill him."

"Wasn't that in a movie about mountain men with Charlton Heston?"

"Yep, and Brian Keith," he said. "I think that's where they got the idea for the scene. Anyway, Colter somehow survived, killing one of the Indians who went after him before escaping from the others. He found his way to Yellowstone and eventually back to civilization."

"Where they didn't believe him?"

My friend nodded. "The running from the Indians part they did, but not the notion of a place that had geysers and bubbling mud. No, they laughed at him until a few other explorers managed to find Yellowstone."

While I took that bit of history in, he jumped right into another bit of trivia, trying to set a foundation for his own story. "Did you know there are those who believe that London was originally named Caer Troia, or New Troy, and founded by a man named Brutus?" he asked. "At least according to old Welsh legend and books by E. O. Gordon and Dunan Wilkins."

He had probably spent years researching it long before he ever said anything about it to his family or friends. Armed with his research, he could offer informed speculation for his critics. "I'm just saying that since time began, soldiers or armies seemed to manage to get everywhere, and I suspect not all of them made it back, including those that went to Vietnam."

He was right. Over the last one thousand years, a large number of soldiers in a variety of armies hadn't made it home. The Chinese knew that for centuries, and the Japanese, French, and we learned it soon enough.

"Did your educated friend give any credence to the 'Proud Mary' part?"

" 'Meant to Mary,' and actually she did. She said that I had that wrong, too. It probably wasn't 'meant to Mary' but more than likely, the Latin phrase, *memento mori*."

"Which is the punch line for this story, right?"

He smiled. "Which means your interviewing skills are getting better. There was hardly the heavy sarcasm in that question that you had in the others. 'Memento Mori' means 'Remember to die.' So how's that for a different war story, Mr. Pulitzer?"

"A floating Roman ghost in Vietnam with a cryptic Latin omen. Yeah, that's different, all right. You sure it wasn't the colonel telling you that Elvis has left the building?"

He ignored my question. "It wasn't so cryptic, really. When you think about it, it means that we all need to be prepared to die one day, and maybe it's more important that we take time to live. I think it's a lesson every soldier since time began learns in combat."

"So it was just a dream, then? A mild hallucination from too much garlic in your C rations?"

"Yeah. Probably. But one that seemed real to me at the time. I'm going to order a salad," he said, looking for the waitress, who was behind the counter. Getting up, he walked toward her. "You want one?" he asked, turning back.

"Sure."

"What kind of salad dressing?"

Seizing the moment, I said, "Caesar."

He stared at me for a moment and then slowly shook his head again. "Caesar, huh? So tell me again, why are we friends?"

"I know the best pizza places and, more important, when I write your story, I have the ability to make you taller, less wrinkled or fat, and considerably more manly."

"Which is why the pen is mightier than the sword."

"Are we talking dessert, too?"

The tall, handsome, and intellectually gifted man nodded and laughed, and when he did, all of the women in the restaurant sighed with desire and wanton lust, even the lesbian couple seated nearby.

THE VISITOR

When Nguyen Tat Thanh paid a visit to the United States in the 1920s, the small, thin former Vietnamese schoolteacher came to learn something firsthand of the "Land of the Free and Home of the Brave."

After all, several of his heroes were the American presidents Thomas Jefferson and Abraham Lincoln. Most of all, Thanh was inspired by the amazing American document that reads: "All men are created equal . . . they are endowed by their creator with certain inalienable rights . . ."—a hope that he held for his own country that was subjugated by France.

When Thanh first read the words of the American Declaration of Independence, he was moved by their passion, strength, and eloquence. He knew that they held just as much significance for a Vietnam occupied by the French as they did for the American colonists who had been oppressed by the British. In fact, he was so inspired, he borrowed those same emphatic words when he was drafting the Declaration of Independence of Vietnam.

In a small rooming house in Brooklyn, New York, and in the city's libraries, he read everything he could on the American Revolution, Jefferson and his times, and the struggles of Lincoln during a war that divided his country. On the streets of New York, he learned something of the American people, who enjoyed the benefits of the long, difficult revolutionary years.

He returned to Europe and eventually his own home country, greatly influenced by what he had learned from a post–World War I France, England, the new Soviet Union, China, and from the streets of the United States, and in particular those of New York City during the "Roaring Twenties."

During the thirty years he traveled the world, learning more of independence movements and revolutions, he went by other names besides Thanh. At times he called himself Nguyen Sing Cung, Nilovsky, Nguyen O Phap, Wang, and Nguyen Ai Quoc, but only after he returned to his native country did he adopt the name that the rest of the world would come to know him by: Ho Chi Minh (He Who Enlightens).

PAYMENT PAST DUE

One of the jobs of a drill instructor in basic training was drilling into a soldier's or a Marine's mind the value of a rifle and what kind of trouble the soldier or Marine would be in without it. In the following story, you'll come to better understand the cost involved with a bottom line measured in more than just dollars and cents.

The measure of man is what he does with power.
—PITTACUS

The rear areas for the field force and combat divisions were boomtowns of logistics and support units. Some were shanty cities containing replacement training areas, sniper schools, NCO academies, finance offices, supply centers, snack bars, and clubs tucked away from the war. Others were far more elaborate and comfortable, with facilities and on-base luxuries that could rival many of the Stateside forts and bases.

The soldier had just been released from the hospital, and at the liaison office, he had been handed a large manila envelope and told to report to Finance before going back to his unit.

"You just need to take care of this first," the liaison

NCO explained to the infantry sergeant, handing him the nine-by-twelve envelope.

"What is it?"

"Routine paperwork," said the staff sergeant. "Here. Let me draw you a map on the back of it and write down the building number," he added, taking back the envelope and writing down the directions.

The stitches pulled against the bandages on the soldier's legs where he had been shot through both thighs. The muscles ached like a son of a bitch. They had atrophied, but he was lucky, and he knew it. They were clean wounds; the machine-gun bullets hadn't hit bone, which was fortunate. The North Vietnamese soldier who shot him was maybe ten to twelve feet away. Had the bullets hit bone, they would have splintered the bones. Instead, they ripped across the thighs, tearing trenches into the flesh and making the soldier feel as though he had been hit with a flaming baseball bat.

Knocked down, bleeding, and shaking in fear, he somehow had managed to return fire, killing the soldier before crawling to the immediate safety of a large tree. As the medic raced up to treat him, the soldier already had his hands on the wounds, trying to use pressure to stop the bleeding as the blood poured between his fingers.

Lifted out by helicopter, the twenty-year-old soldier was flown to a field hospital, where the wounds were treated but not closed. Then he was flown out again, to a rear area evacuation hospital, and operated on.

Afterward, he was placed in a surgical ward, and his stitched wounds were cleaned once a day with hydrogen peroxide to avoid infection. In Vietnam, the infection rate was abnormally high, so the wounded soldier went through the same grisly ritual for seven days.

The following week was spent getting him back on his feet. Because the wounds weren't serious wounds—as wounds went in Vietnam—he would go through physical therapy and return to his unit. At each session, the physical therapist repeatedly bent the legs to get them to move, as the soldier winced in pain. Progress was slow and painful, but it came.

By the time he had been told to report to Finance, he was getting around with the help of a cane. Finding the one-story, wooden-plank structure with corrugated tin roof in a row of similar structures took some doing. When he located it, he double-checked the building number on the piece of paper against the small, official-looking sign next to the door and, satisfied it was correct, hobbled in beyond the screen door. He wasn't sure why he was there. He had just been told to report to the office.

He leaned on a cane for support as he walked, waddling like a duck. Back at his unit's base camp, he would receive rehabilitation for the legs; the doctors at the evacuation hospital said as much, and he suspected that it would be just as painful as the physical therapy he had received at the evacuation hospital. But that would come later. He still had to get there. But first he needed to jump through the army's hoops.

The screen door of the office opened slowly as the sergeant limped on in. The spring-operated door slammed against the frame behind him. The distinctive crack caught the attention and disdain of both the specialist five and warrant officer who manned the office.

"Spring's too tight is all it is, sir," the specialist five said, frowning as he got up from his chair, came around the counter, and—ignoring the sergeant—began to pull on the spring, twisting and stretching it until he was certain he had adjusted the tension.

"There!" he said, back to the infantry sergeant, who didn't seem to care one way or another. The young sergeant didn't look like an FNG (fucking new guy), but his fatigues and jungle boots were brand-new. Often, you could tell how long someone had been in country by the sun-bleached uniform and scraped leather of their boots. If it hadn't been for the soldier's deep tan and the Combat Infantryman's Badge pinned just above his left pocket, the clerk would have left him standing there for a little longer. New guys were never in a hurry, anyway, because they had too much time to do.

"So how can I help you, Sarge?" he said, walking back around the counter and back into the base of his power. Since they were both paygrade E-5, the counter and the office gave the specialist five the distinct edge, and he knew it. It was his domain, and his authority was almost palpable.

"Division Supply said I needed to come over here and take care of this," the sergeant said, handing the clerk the envelope he had been given earlier. The specialist five clerk ripped it open, removed the contents, and then read them over quickly.

"No problem," the clerk said, more to himself than to the sergeant. He walked over to a bank of filing cabinets that was arranged against the back wall, opened a middle drawer to the cabinet on the end, and retrieved the form he was looking for.

"Here we go!" he said. There was no expression on his face when he walked back, slapped the new piece of paper on the counter, and in rapid succession said, "You need to print your name here; your social security number here; the amount you want deducted here; then sign it *here*," he said, marking four Xs near the blocks he wanted the sergeant to fill in and sign. The clerk handed the sergeant a black pen and a warning. "Don't leave with my pen, either."

"What is this?" the infantry sergeant asked, scanning the new form.

"An allotment form."

"Why do I need an allotment form?"

The specialist five looked at the sergeant as if he was stupid or a grunt, which the clerk believed were the same thing. He wasn't alone in thinking that if grunts had any brains then they wouldn't be grunts. Not in that war or any other one. He breathed in slowly and exhaled loudly like an impatient teacher trying to make a point to a student who wasn't intelligent enough to grasp the concept. "It's to pay for the rifle you lost," he said, pointing to the envelope. "Didn't Supply tell you?"

"No," said the sergeant, more than a little confused.

"Well, they should have. Anyway, you'll want to put in the amount of money you want taken out of your monthly paycheck in the box I've marked. Otherwise, they'll take it all at once, which means you won't see a paycheck for a month or two."

The sergeant stared at the form and then back at the clerk as his eyes narrowed and his voice took on a distinctive edge. "I'm not signing this form. I'm not paying for a rifle I didn't lose!" he said, which only caused the clerk to step back and wait for the sergeant to blow off the steam before he gave him one last chance to sign. If he didn't, then the grunt could go screw himself for all he cared.

The office was small, maybe twelve feet by twelve feet, with four official-looking desks, desk lamps, half-filled in-baskets, and the bank of filing cabinets. There was just enough room for the counter and a small, plastic rotating fan on the other end, which droned indifferently even as the tone of the office took a decidedly cold turn.

When he spoke again, the specialist five's voice no

longer concealed his sarcasm. "Personally, I don't give a shit what happened to the rifle. Lost or whatever. You signed for it. You lost it. So now you have to pay for it. It's that simple; so either it's monthly installment payments or all of the money will be taken out at once. It's your call, Sarge!"

"But I didn't lose my rifle. I got shot and medevacked out. Hell, I just got out of the hospital less than an hour and a half ago!"

The clerk shrugged. Sure the grunt sergeant had a cane, but that still didn't mean anything.

"This is bullshit! I ain't signing the fucking form!" the sergeant said. His loud words brought the warrant officer out of his seat and into the argument.

"At ease!" the warrant officer yelled, taking control in a command voice that both understood.

"This is stupid!" said the sergeant.

"I said, at ease! Now, what's your problem, Sergeant?"

The grunt turned away from the warrant officer, mumbled something, and then turned back glaring at the officer. There was no way he was going to win, and he knew it.

"My problem, sir?" said the infantry sergeant, carefully weighing his words and knowing the careful balance between criticism and insubordination. "My problem is that you people are punishing me for getting wounded by trying to get me to pay for a rifle I didn't lose."

The warrant officer's eyes went from the grunt to the cane, and then back to the form. "It says the weapon you were issued was reported as 'lost.' Not as a 'combat loss,' which is what it would be if you were medevacked out," the warrant officer said, reading over the division supply form. "You signed for the weapon. You apparently lost it, so you will, in fact, have to pay for the weapon."

"This is crazy!" the grunt sergeant said, in protest. He turned in a half circle, winced from the pain in his legs, and then clenched his teeth. "I get wounded in combat, medevacked out, operated on two weeks ago or so, and now I gotta deal with this! I don't fucking believe it."

"Where were you wounded?" the warrant officer asked with a certain amount of skepticism.

The grunt sergeant pointed to his lap. "I was shot in both thighs. Here and here," he said, going from his front thigh and half turning to show the back of his left leg.

"Then how come you're still in Vietnam?" said the specialist five, knowing he had caught the sergeant in the big lie; people who get shot go home. Everybody knew that.

"Through and through," the sergeant replied, bitterly. It didn't mean anything to the clerk, while the warrant officer listened on with a new interest. "Flesh wounds. The bullets didn't hit any bones. They only severed muscles and flesh, so I didn't get sent home."

"When were you wounded?" asked the specialist five.

"Three weeks ago. You can check with my unit or the hospital. They were nice enough to sew me up with metal wire, give me a cane, and send me back on my way. Now, to add insult to injury, you people want me to pay for the rifle that was taken away from me on the medevac helicopter. Get on a landline and call them! Go ahead!"

The grunt sergeant could see there was still some hesitation in the warrant officer's eyes, so the sergeant fumbled with his jungle uniform trouser pants. "You don't believe me?"

"Hey! What are you doing?" yelled the specialist five as

the sergeant dropped his trousers and revealed the thick gauze bandages covering the wounds to the upper thighs.

"I got hit here first with an AK-47 round. It was like getting hit with a baseball bat, and then it burned," the sergeant explained, pointing to his right thigh, "and then I got shot here a few minutes later, which ripped out the back of my left leg. Like I said, they sewed it up with wire stitches, so I get them out, I'll start physical therapy, and then go back to my unit in the field," he added. While the right bandage was relatively thick, white and clean, the heavier left bandage showed the reddish-yellow discolor from the seeping wound where the stitches had worked loose.

"Pull up your pants," said the warrant officer, and turning back to the specialist five said, "Combat loss the weapon."

"We haven't checked out his story?" asked the clerk.

"Combat loss it," he said again without further explanation. The clerk was upset that the warrant officer overrode his decision but got some degree of satisfaction back when the warrant officer turned on the infantry sergeant. "You won't have to pay for the rifle, Sergeant, but let's make one thing perfectly clear here," he said, menacingly. "You don't come in my office and give my people a hard time for doing their job, and you certainly don't rant and rave at them either. You understand me?"

"Yes, sir," said the sergeant, quietly.

"Good. Now you can leave," said the warrant officer, dismissing the soldier, who thought about saying "Thank you" but instead said, "Yes, sir" again, then turned around and limped away.

"Take care of your rifle, or next time you will pay!" the specialist five yelled after the grunt, who didn't bother to respond.

THE PRICE OF COMBAT

This story has a happy ending, at least for the veterans involved, but I don't think telling you this will spoil it for you. It is a story of personal ethics and what it takes to define and soothe a conscience. If anything, the story will offer at least one answer to the question What price glory?

Oddly enough, since this story first appeared, I've had two veterans call to say that they made similar discoveries and recoveries.

Virtue is insufficient temptation.
—George Bernard Shaw

It was a military reunion, and the veteran agreed to tell his story at a small, quiet hotel bar. We sat in a booth next to a plate-glass window that overlooked the far, blue Olympic Mountains. A faded orange tint from the sunset gave the twilight evening sky its last hint of color.

A mutual friend had thought I would be interested in listening to what the storyteller had to say, so over constant coffee, we went through the identification preliminaries, which to Vietnam veterans means talking first about whom we had served with, which divisions, and where and when. It was a ritual with most veterans, and we weren't exempt. With the groundwork set, we were ready.

The sound of Kenny G's alto sax was being pumped in over the sound system, and there was a flow to the music that made it conducive to talk. "It was the second week in May of 1970," explained the veteran, "less than two weeks after we made the raid into Cambodia. We started out of Tay Ninh and moved so fast we caught the Viet Cong and the North Vietnamese Army literally with their pants down and their dicks in their hands. We had a chance to kick ass, so we did." The veteran wasn't telling me anything I didn't already know, but I let the background material slide because I wanted to see what it uncovered. I took another sip of coffee and stared out the window, watching a seagull make lazy circles in the twilight sky. So far, the path was well worn and familiar; it was common history. Most "war stories" demand a point of reference, and to other vets, it's their own memories that serve as the guide.

It was no secret that for years prior to the invasion, a border war was carried out by the North Vietnamese Army and the Viet Cong, who operated openly in the neighboring nation. The Viet Cong's headquarters unit was there, as were entire divisions of brand-new soldiers who had come down the Ho Chi Minh trail to fight the war in the south.

U.S. Forces special operations groups and other raids were conducted in response to the attacks, and "For the record" denials came from Hanoi and Washington D.C., with both sides adamantly swearing they didn't have combat troops in Cambodia, nor were they conducting cross-border raids.

"The Ho Chi Minh trail was temporarily closed. It was amazing how many people in the United States believed the North Vietnamese when they said they weren't operating in Cambodia or Laos."

"It was all bullshit," the veteran said, "because now we know the NVA and Viet Cong had thousands of soldiers and hundreds of elaborate and well-stocked bases in Cambodia and our air force was secretly bombing the crap out of them with the approval of the Cambodian government, who were swearing to the Vietnamese they didn't know anything about it.

"Everybody was doing it to each other and lying about it publicly," he said, adding that after May of 1970, when South Vietnamese and American forces invaded the enemy bases, the pretense was over.

"It wasn't really an invasion," he said, while I nodded.

"I know, it was just a raid that would last for sixty-one days and go maybe twenty miles plus because of politics," I said.

"But at least it would end the lying and half-truths for a while. For us, it was a chance to clean house on the enemy units who kept crossing the border to hit us and then racing back when we went after them."

I nodded again.

We talked further of the NVA and the Viet Cong intelligence sections who didn't believe the raid would happen, even when the American units began massing men and equipment in the base camps along the primary infiltration routes. We agreed they had to believe it was a bluff; their best strategists must have known it would be political suicide for the American president because the American public, already tired and disenchanted, wouldn't stand for it!

Only it did happen. President Richard M. Nixon ordered the attack, and the North Vietnamese Army and the Viet Cong units were hastily trying to pull back far-

ther into the Cambodian countryside to get away from
the Americans, who had the momentum.

In the first few hours, the massive bombing runs from
the continuous flights of B-52 aircraft from bases in
neighboring Thailand and the gunship attacks from the
Cav's deadly Cobra helicopters, out of the bordering
Vietnamese provinces, had accounted for thousands of
enemy casualties. These were no inflated body counts
coming from rear-area public affairs officers, either, but
firsthand accounts of line after line of shattered fighting
positions and gutted, burning vehicles and equipment
along dirt roads littered with rotting corpses. Huge
caches of equipment and supplies lay exposed in the aftermath, verifying that it was indeed a victory for the
Americans and their allies.

Elements of the 25th Infantry Division, the 11th Ar-
mored Cavalry Regiment, the 9th Infantry Division, and
the 1st Air Cavalry Division had conducted a lightning-
quick operation that had caught the enemy by surprise,
and they were taking full advantage of the military opportunity.

Millions of rounds of ammunition and literally hundreds of thousands of rockets and antiaircraft rounds
were captured by the Americans and South Vietnamese
Army, along with tons of food, vehicles, uniforms,
equipment, and documents. In one jungle base camp
alone, there were nearly twelve thousand enemy bunkers
and fighting positions.

Viet Cong and North Vietnamese Army units were literally leaving tons of equipment and weapons behind, at
times fleeing only seconds before the American reconnaissance units arrived. Battling it out to the inevitable
end as the invading forces rolled up and over them, the
pockets of resistance believed the Americans wouldn't

cross the border. But they finally had, and with a vengeance.

It would take a while before the North Vietnamese Army and Viet Cong units could regroup and conduct their own bitter counterattacks, so for the moment, the Americans and the allies had the edge.

That's when the veteran worked his way into his story, weaving the two together into his personal tapestry. "Our reconnaissance platoon had fought another small, dirty fight for another Viet Cong bunker complex. It was our fifth such fight in as many days. The Viet Cong were trying to hold on to this one a little harder than the others, but they weren't having much luck.

"We had the OH-6 scout observation helicopters flying low over the trees, hitting them from the sky, while we moved in underneath the jungle canopy. Then, when we hit a pocket of resistance, we called in our gunships, and they tore into the holdouts with rockets and automatic machine-gun fire. We called it minigun fire, but it was really just the Gatling-gun concept updated for the sixties. It fired five or six thousand rounds a minute, and we were hitting them hard and fast."

The veteran explained that enemy soldiers were surrendering in clusters, while others died, stubbornly defending their positions. As the Americans advanced, the full extent of their finds was becoming known. Interlocked fighting positions and strategic bunkers of handhewn logs and packed earth formed a perimeter protecting hidden jungle fortresses and villagelike havens. Whole jungle cities were being found, and the veteran and his fellow soldiers had discovered themselves in one such setting that someone overflying the large complex dubbed "The City."

But kicking ass was taking its toll, and the American

platoon was a little less than enthusiastic about the discovery. Their ragged edges were beginning to show. There had also been a question about why the point squad hadn't been rotated off the dangerous lead. The unit's first sergeant said that was because the point squad was the most experienced. Period.

The veteran was a twenty-one-year-old buck sergeant (E-5) at the time and a squad leader for the point squad. "We were getting screwed for being good at what we did. I tried arguing with the first sergeant, asking just how in the fuck did he think the rest of the squads would get any experience if they kept us on point all the damn time?

"His argument was to say that we were the best he had, so we were getting punished for being good. Taking the lead every day was wearing us down. The Viet Cong knew we were coming, so it was like walking into an ambush knowing you were the target. They were in the bunkers, and they had everything to lose, and we were the ones who were taking it away from them.

"The going was slow, deliberate. Once inside a bunker complex, though, everything changed. We sprinted from fighting position to fighting position, scurrying for cover while covering our buddies as we moved. Man, it was like Christmas! Inside The City we were finding a little bit of everything—trucks, cars, motorcycles, and enough stores and equipment to man an army, but then the army that owned it was in the process of leaving it behind.

"Another unit moving from another side even found a Volkswagen bug parked next to a bamboo garage. It was a real city, and within outdoor kitchens and storage bunkers, we found hastily abandoned AK-47s and every other piece of equipment you can imagine. A small road concealed by canopied vegetation wound around structures and dwellings that formed the enemy base camp.

There were outdoor kitchens, half-underground, with well-worn steps carved out of the packed orange clay, and on the open stoves, you could see rice cooking and some sort of big bird roasting over an open spit. The main thrust of the battle, what there was of it, was over, but there was still the mop-up operation," he said.

"We were clearing out the bunkers one at a time. We had already cleared ten or so bunkers, but three of them were still occupied by Viet Cong soldiers who weren't about to surrender. So we would drop a grenade in one opening, yell 'Fire in the hole!' and when it exploded, follow up by jumping inside and finishing up the hard-core little bastards.

"Finally, we ran into a large elaborate bunker that had log braces and sandbagged supports that told us we had something different here. There was a bamboo door that was half opened, and we could make out shadows moving inside.

"We tried talking them out, only they fired back through the door, and they even tossed out one of their grenades at us, a small Chinese thing that looked like one of the old German potato mashers. Unlike the kind the Germans used during World War II, the Chinese version was designed to mess you up instead of kill you. I heard somewhere they figured it would take several other soldiers to carry out the wounded and that they all made better targets because of it. Anyway, after it exploded, we tossed in a few of our own, and before the dust cleared, we locked and loaded and blew them away.

"I was the first one in, and just inside the door I found a dead Viet Cong officer seated on the floor, his hand still holding his unfired Makarov pistol. I kicked away the pistol to make sure he was dead and then looked around the small bunker. My eyes were slowly adjusting to the dim light, and all I was really looking for were the shadows. I saw four or five large canvas bags, which I mistook for dead enemy soldiers, and then after I shot them, blowing some of their stuffing out, I recognized them for what they were. Finally, I found the second guy dead behind a small counter; half of his head had been blown away by the grenades. Next to him was his AK-47 assault rifle with several magazines loaded and lying in a neat little row like he was going to play John Wayne and hold down the Alamo. It was over. The two dead holdouts were the only ones.

"I yelled 'All clear!' to the others and turned back to look around the room. Three of the four walls were lined with shelves, and there was a small desk. But it was the canvas bags that really caught my attention. It took a few seconds for it to register, and even then I couldn't believe it! The bags were filled with money!"

The veteran's eyes grew wide, and a half smile formed on his mouth. "U.S. greenbacks, South Vietnamese dong, and even French francs. It was a Viet Cong bank.

"Meanwhile, the first sergeant was on the radio, asking what we had, saying that G-2 wanted to know if we had any intelligence data like maps or papers, so I told the radioman to tell him we were still clearing the bunkers. We had some maps we pulled out of another bunker, so I told him to say that we had maps and we'd drive them out in the fucking Volkswagen if that's what he wanted! We didn't tell them about the money because we figured that wouldn't be intelligent. If anything, it might only tell the intelligence people what dumb shits we were. Money talks, but nobody ever said it could hold a decent conversation!

"I think that's when we got the idea to keep it! We didn't have much time since everybody and his brother were landing their helicopters to see the extent of the bunker complex, so we loaded up our rucksacks. When we finally made it back to the rear area, we figured out a way to bring it back to the States.

"There were five of us, and it was a mutual decision, so we, well . . . we kept it."

I guess I looked morally outraged, but it was really my standard look of envy.

"You think we're thieves, right?"

I shook my head. "No," I said. "You can't steal something that officially wasn't there. The Viet Cong and the North Vietnamese Army said they were never in Cambodia. Besides, there are no more Viet Cong. The North Vietnamese edged them out when they took over after the war anyway. They screwed them royally."

The veteran shrugged. "Our rationale was different. We knew there wouldn't be any parades or pats on the back for Vietnam service and that nobody really gave a shit about us anyway. The people on the left said we were all *baby killers*, while those on the right thought we weren't fighting hard enough because we were the first Americans to lose a war."

"The second, actually," I said. "We lost the War of 1812. The British won, but they just got tired and went home."

"Are you sure?" he asked. I nodded.

"Reasonably."

"Anyway, we knew the Viet Cong didn't get the U.S. dollars legally and that it was more than likely black market profits. So we didn't look upon it as stealing. If anything, it was booty, the spoils of war. The stuff of pirates and kings."

It wasn't hardened perception as much as it was a simple understanding of the times. Returning veterans *were* jeered at and spat upon and harassed by a less than grateful public. I had known others who had found Vietnamese currency or U.S. dollars in hastily abandoned backpacks or bunkers. They had kept it as well, often with the blessing of the platoon sergeants. It was never all that much money—at least it was never reported to be all that much at the time.

The storyteller's voice was rising with anger. "The civilians didn't take the bumps and bruises, and the older veterans didn't understand the politics of this new war. They hadn't lived in the swamps and jungles breathing in mosquitoes or contracting malaria and afterward vomiting their guts out until it seemed like their toes would turn inside out. They hadn't struggled under the weight of a dead buddy's body bag or fought on in numbed resignation for a poorly defined cause!

"Taking the money wasn't stealing," he said again, "because we earned it, a Purple Heart, a body bag, and a miserable day at a time. We paid for it in ways most people could never imagine, so we decided to get something back. There it is!" the veteran said with finality.

I took a drink of my coffee and mulled it over. When I asked how much money they had recovered, the veteran just laughed.

"Enough," he said.

Even after all these years, he didn't feel comfortable sharing his secret with anyone outside of their immediate circle.

I asked if it was as much as one point man found in another incident similar to this, a point man who later sued the army to keep the half million dollars he had found in another jungle bank. The storyteller smiled.

The veteran shook his head again and laughed. "Let's just say a lottery number drafted me into the service, as was the case of the others in the squad. We just made them winning numbers."

When I asked if he or any of the others felt maybe they should have taken the matter to court like the other veteran who sued, the veteran grunted and said, "He lost the case, as I recall. The army kept the money."

I nodded, remembering the outcome as well. The court decided that since the soldier was working for the army at the time of the discovery, it was therefore the employer's property. The government kept it.

"And we know the government wouldn't waste it, don't we?" he said. "So, how about another cup of coffee."

"Sure," I said. "I'll buy."

"No," he said, smiling. "I got it. I can afford it."

THE NIGHTMARE

Ever been frightened by a bad dream? Scared to death by a nightmare that seemed so real you were afraid to go back to sleep for fear you'd have the same dream again? Or afraid that what you dreamed would somehow take life and come out of the shadows after you? Welcome to a nightmare in Vietnam, one that a scout helicopter pilot found himself trembling at until the sun came up the following morning, then trembling even more at the thought of sunset.

All our knowledge has its origins in our perceptions.
—LEONARDO DA VINCI

Tay Ninh Province, 1970
Apache Troop, 1st Squadron, 9th Cavalry

It was the dry season, and there wasn't much of a breeze. Even well past midnight, the temperature in remote Tay Ninh Province hovered somewhere in the high eighties. The humidity was something else entirely, and on his cot in the scout pilots' hootch in his underwear, the young warrant officer was coated with a light layer of sweat. He kicked away the poncho liner he was using as a blanket and turned his pillow over to ease into the cool, cotton mattress cover. Better, he thought, but he knew it wouldn't last; soon the cover would heat up, and then he would have to repeat the process. A bead of sweat trickled down his forehead, around his earlobe, and onto the pillow. It was another long night made longer by the heat.

Somewhere in the distance, the *whumph* of exploding artillery rounds formed a backbeat to the drone of a mosquito that bobbed and weaved around his head in the dark.

Idly slapping at the sound, Bill McIntosh hadn't bothered to look up to see if he had hit the damn thing. It didn't really matter. Even if he had, sooner or later another would find a way through the wire-mesh screen window. Maybe it was just a subconscious gesture he had acquired over the first few months of being in country. Like the war, you kept slapping at it, trying to push away the inevitable.

He swore to himself, turned on his back, and stared at the open rafters in the ceiling, certain that throughout the country there were many little wars like his going on with the besieged experiencing the same frustration. He closed his eyes again and once more tried to get some sleep.

In a few hours, he'd get up and prepare for another mission, another run over the area of operations where he had been shot down five times already in his tour. Three in one month alone. Maybe it wasn't the heat and his tiny tormentor keeping him awake after all.

Absentmindedly, he fingered the scar on the side of his face where the AK-47 round had settled in his teeth after rifling through the small observation helicopter, up across his "chicken plate" protective armor, and through his cheek. Helicopter hell! The OH-6 Loaches were little more than tiny Plexiglas-and-metal lures, dangling at treetop level to draw enemy fire so the observer could mark their position with a smoke grenade. Then the gunship that was circling at three thousand feet above would swoop down and hammer the enemy. But the lure often had scars where the prey had bitten before being gunned down.

Some job. Just your average game of tag, but in this case the one who was it was a ridiculously low and easy target for even the worst shot. The enemy soldier didn't have to be Sergeant Nguyen York to be able to place a couple of bursts into the light observation helicopters at that range. All he had to do was take quick aim and pull the trigger. One round in the fuel tank and *whoosh! boom!* the helicopter exploded into a fireball.

"Crispy critters" they called it when the crews of the scout helicopters, burned beyond recognition, lay huddled in fetal positions, charred and lifeless.

Not that the scout helicopters were unarmed. McIntosh had Sp. Terry Delorme for his machine gunner, and "Mugsy," as he was better known, was pretty damn good at his job. So was David Ham, the big Hawaiian, his observer, with his grenades and M-16 always ready.

They worked in unison. McIntosh would slip the small helicopter to the side when they drew fire so Delorme could return fire immediately while Ham quickly tossed out a red smoke grenade before opening fire as well. Meanwhile McIntosh would pull out of the line of fire before the Cobra gunship roared down from the heavens and introduced the North Vietnamese Army soldiers to a new version of hell.

Five hundred hours was enough to get him out of the scouts, at least that was the troop's policy. Five hundred hours would earn the pilot a safer job. But less than one third of the Troop's scout pilots ever made it that far. McIntosh wasn't sure how he had made it to the five-hundred-hour mark and now, working on seven hundred hours, wasn't certain why he stayed. Maybe it had to do with the fact that he was good at his job and that, somewhere along the way, he had begun to like it. He and his two-man crew had killed, officially, over 150 enemy soldiers from less than a hundred yards away and were responsible for hundreds of others being wounded. Minimac, as he was better known, was a competent professional killer, but his success was beginning to take its toll.

Well above the cutoff, McIntosh remained in the Scout Platoon because the platoon needed experienced scout pilots, and he couldn't let the new pilots take over the job. They wouldn't last. They would do something stupid, and that would be it for them and the entire crew. Besides, there weren't all that many new pilots arriving to fill the slots of those who had been killed. In flight school, more than one newly pinned pilot was warned against going into the Cav's premier reconnaissance unit, the 1st of the 9th. The warnings were blunt: "They're the Cav's cowboys, and they're always at the forefront of combat."

That was true. The 1st Air Cavalry Division had accounted for half of the enemy casualties in the war, and the 1st of the 9th led the division.

Maybe when a few more of the new guys got experience, then he'd step down. Yeah, maybe then, too, his hands would stop shaking whenever he thought about the near misses.

McIntosh slapped at the buzzing again, thinking that maybe one of these days he'd walk into the Old Man's office and say he'd had enough. Yeah, one of these days, he thought, drifting off to an uncomfortable sleep.

If it wasn't the sweltering Vietnamese heat, then it was the bad dreams. Nothing surreal, just vivid and plausible nightmares. Like finding himself hovering over the bomb crater, waiting to extract a gut-shot infantryman, and suddenly finding himself face-to-face with an NVA soldier, a gook with an RPG-7, smiling as he leveled the shoulder-fired rocket at the Plexiglas bubble cockpit. McIntosh couldn't do anything but hold the helicopter's controls or crash as he stared into the face of his executioner, and the man pulled the rocket launcher's trigger.

In another, it was taking fire and losing altitude as the controls were wrenched from the dying helicopter by too many bullets and too much gravity, crashing through the trees and finding himself trapped in the burning wreckage. Struggling to free himself, only to see an enemy soldier staring at him intently while leveling a rifle at the aircraft and emptying the thirty-round clip in a sustained burst.

McIntosh bolted upright, dodging the phantom rounds, heart pounding, wondering when the nightmares would go away. From time to time, he wondered whether his conscience was paying penance or simply extracting its due.

A creaking noise sounded, as though the hootch's screen was opening and closing slowly. Maybe it was his imagination. In combat settings, after disturbed sleep, small noises were often amplified by the imagination. The noise was faint but enough to stir him from his anguished thoughts.

There was still no breeze, but the distant artillery batteries fell silent so early in the morning. The whine of a generator near the tactical operations center offered another clue to the distraction as bad dream after bad dream bled from one to another with fluid finality.

Predawn nightmares never made it easy to get back to

sleep. He had wanted to see a doctor about it, but what then? At best, he'd be grounded, and that was worse than getting shot down.

The small pilot, who looked like someone's younger brother playing army, flipped the pillow over one more time and turned on his side, facing the small room's only door. He was drifting off again just as the shadow in the darkened doorway moved. Somebody else couldn't sleep either.

The hootch housed several other pilots, so it was probably one of them heading to the latrine outside. But the man didn't go outside; the dark figure stood quietly in McIntosh's doorway. The veteran scout pilot didn't believe in ghosts, but the small, dark figure seemed to appear from nowhere, standing over the bed like an ominous apparition.

The scout pilot wanted to ask just what in the fuck the stupid son of a bitch thought he was doing, when he suddenly realized it wasn't an American. He tried to scream but couldn't find the voice. If he yelled, would the shadow soldier kill him or simply disappear? If it was only a nightmare, then what would he tell the other pilots when they came running to see what was the matter? Another nightmare? "Get a grip, you crazy asshole!" they'd say, swear again, and go back to sleep.

Like most other frontline soldiers working and living in the border region who slept with loaded weapons close at hand, McIntosh kept a .38 pistol at one edge of his bed while a large bolo knife lay sheathed, inches from his right hand. But if he reached for either one, he would give away the fact he was awake.

The shadow moved again, placing something down carefully and bumping the door frame as he did. That was enough to tell the scout pilot it wasn't a ghost or a bad dream. He could smell the warm, musky odor of the sweating intruder mixed with *nuoc mam*, the pungent Vietnamese fish sauce.

In an instant of understanding, McIntosh yanked the large knife from its resting place and leaped at the darkened figure, swinging the blade in a wide arc with all of his strength. And missed. The wiry Vietnamese leaped away as the blade fell, and then charged the American, hitting him at the chest and driving them both into the hootch's plywood wall.

The scout pilot felt the man's left hand reach up to try to stop the knife as McIntosh brought it down hard against the man's neck and shoulder. Only there wasn't a neck and shoulder.

McIntosh swung again, hitting the plywood wall a second time, realizing there was no desperate struggle. No enemy soldier. Just another nightmare.

"Jesus H. Christ! McIntosh!" a voice yelled from down the hallway. "Knock that shit off!" the voice added angrily as another awakened pilot turned on a light, only to find the veteran scout in his underwear, lying on the floor, sweating, shaking, and still clutching the bolo knife.

Seconds later, machine-gun fire and sudden explosions brought the second pilot to the floor. Outside, the base camp was erupting in a close, vicious firefight.

"What the . . . ?" they said before the piercing cry echoed across the troop's compound.

"Gooks in the wire! Gooks in the wire!" someone was shouting above the din of battle. Bright orange flashes mushroomed and instantly disappeared outside the screen door, followed by thundering blasts.

Scrambling for his pistol while the second pilot scurried away to retrieve his own weapon, McIntosh inched up the darkened hallway toward the hootch's door. Moments later, he was joined by the second pilot, who had found an AK-47 assault rifle.

"Don't fire that thing until you're sure of a target, otherwise our own people are going to shoot the shit out of us. You hear me?" McIntosh said.

The second pilot nodded. "What the fuck's going on?" he asked.

McIntosh shrugged, looking for the blood on his hands, that somehow had turned to sweat. "Sapper attack more than likely. The gooks slipped through the barbed wire and into the camp."

Base security was good, and the units effectively drove the North Vietnamese Army units and Viet Cong cadre deeper into the jungles, but bases were probed periodically. Almost nightly, mortar or rocket attacks had replaced the ground probes in the province, yet occasional sapper or enemy commando infiltration teams still caused considerable trouble. The sapper team objectives were straightforward enough—blow up American helicopters and artillery and, in the process, kill as many Americans as possible.

McIntosh was scraped and bruised from his surreal ordeal, but other than that, he was okay. Outside, though, the real war was catching up to his nightmares. In the compound area, soldiers were running toward the long, wood, and tin-roofed hootch, using it as protective cover as they bounded toward the flight line where the fighting seemed to be the heaviest.

"What's going on?" McIntosh asked one of the Recon Platoon's sergeants, who turned, his M-16 rifle at the ready position, aiming over the pilot's shoulder as he recognized the warrant officers. The young sergeant wasn't taking any chances.

"Sappers!" the sergeant said, turning his attention

back to the flight line. "We've got five or so dead gooks in the troop area, and we're trying to flush out the rest. We're searching for them now. Stay inside and stay down."

The two pilots nodded, looked around warily, and eased back inside the hootch. McIntosh checked his room again and, still not finding any trace of an intruder, breathed a little easier. Or tried to.

It had been just a dream after all, but the real nightmare was still going on at the flight line. Sunrise was still several hours away, and finding and destroying the rest of the enemy sapper team wouldn't be easy. Still, they had been compromised; the element of surprise was gone. It would be up to the Recon Platoon, military police, and grunts to rout them out.

By late morning, ten of the eleven-man enemy unit had been killed or captured, with the search continuing for the final intruder. Speculation had it that the eleventh man had escaped, but nobody was taking any unnecessary chances. Soldiers walked to the outhouses and showers, openly carrying their weapons, and heavily armed MPs roamed the base with purpose. In combat, it didn't take long to realize that carelessness or stupidity could easily get you killed.

"He got away, huh?" McIntosh said to himself uneasily when he heard the news.

"Yeah. He's probably hauling ass back toward Hanoi by now," someone added. McIntosh wasn't laughing. His thoughts and focus were elsewhere, not beyond the barbed wire or even out in the dense jungle of the province but on a war that was much closer and more costly to fight.

His tour of duty and his physical war would continue for several more months, and during those drawn-out days, the warrant officer would fly dangerous scout missions through volleys of enemy machine guns and small arms. To the casual observer, he seemed unafraid, but at night, when alone in his hootch and close to his bolo knife and pistol, the nightmares would stalk him until sunrise. Every squeak and shadow was the eleventh man in a forever war.

As a scout pilot with Apache Troop, the 1st of the 9th Cavalry, Bill McIntosh was shot down six times. Once, after saving an encircled infantry squad by repeatedly landing his small helicopter in an impossible landing zone and extracting the trapped soldiers, there was talk about nominating him for the Medal of Honor. Nothing came of it, but McIntosh won the respect of those he served with and those he rescued.

Today, he lives in the Pacific Northwest, and while his war has been over for well over twenty years, the thought of sunset still leaves him apprehensive.

FINDING RELIGION

There are some who say it is easy to find God in war; at the boiling point of battle when the heat becomes overwhelming, any hope of salvation and survival comes in turning your fate over to a higher power, even if it isn't the one you intended to find.

It is conceivable that religion may be morally useful without being intellectually sustainable.
—JOHN STUART MILL

It was the rainy season, and the North Vietnamese Army rocket artillery regiment was using the cover of the monsoons to move rocket crews into position. When they were ready, they sent the barrage of 122mm rockets and 81mm mortar rounds into the military base, concentrating on the U.S. Marines in particular.

It was no secret that the NVA hated the Marines and struck out at them at any opportunity. The monsoons provided such an opportunity; the heavy wind and rain kept the American helicopters grounded, while the Marines remained in their tents, hootches, fighting positions, and bunkers, hunkered down, trying to stay dry.

With targets fixed and charted, the NVA aligned portable rocket launchers and mortar tubes and fired off a quick volley before hurriedly moving on to another location to repeat the process before they could take any return fire.

The Marine artillery zeroed in on the original firing site shortly after the first rounds exploded, then switched to other likely sites. The NVA, however, had learned how to successfully attack the American bases at sites of their own choosing and at their own schedule. In hit-and-run attacks, they'd drop their mortars or fire their rockets into the bases and camps. The NVA gunners didn't have to mutter "Ducks in a barrel" to understand the concept.

After being bombarded for a week, Marines took to referring to the base as "Ground Zero," "Rocket City," or "Rocket Alley," and the ordeal of incoming rockets and mortars gave new status to the camp.

Thundering explosions turned parked aircraft and hootches into shredded debris and sent the Marines scrambling for the dark, dank safety of underground bunkers. Fifty years after World War I, the Marines were still involved in trench warfare, up to their ankles and asses in an orange Asian ooze.

Once the steady rain began to pool, small trickles and rivulets turned into consistent streams. Rats and snakes, forced from their hiding places and looking for drier ground, sought refuge with the Marines in the dark underground bunkers. Drainage was a constant problem, and long after the storm had passed, many of the bunkers held more than a few inches of stagnant, brown water. As it rained, the water level rose in the bunkers until the Marines were standing knee deep in the water as rockets and mortars exploded above them.

During the bombardment, one Marine began losing it, the cracks in his bravado becoming noticeable. He had been through one too many shellings, and he'd simply had enough. The heavy pounding from the enemy rockets and mortars, combined with the uncertainty of hurriedly climbing down into a watery pit filled with stagnant water and unpleasant slithery surprises, had done it. This new attack was the final straw.

There were maybe five or six Marines in the bunker. Most were shifting uncomfortably, waiting for the attack to end so they could return to their bunks. Several were smoking, and most were bored, except for the man who was losing it. As each explosion sent a new layer of dust over the bunker's occupants and the already muddy water, the frightened Marine laughed nervously. As the explosions moved closer, the lanky lance corporal began to cry and laugh intermittently, making the others who were in the underground shelter even more uncomfortable.

"Take it easy, man," someone said to the lance corporal. "They're aiming mostly at the guns. Mostly," he said again, as an enemy rocket tore into their company area.

"You don't understand!" the lance corporal screamed in a less than convincing voice. His hands were gesturing wildly, and even in the dim light, it was easy to see that his eyes were darting back and forth from the Marines in the bunker to the opening in the bunker and the noise outside.

"Understand what?"

"We're causing this, you know? All of us! We're bringing this on ourselves!" he yelled, while someone in the rear of the shelter told him to "shut the fuck up!"

"I know why this is happening!" he said, wildly excited at his discovery. "I really do! I know why! I know why!"

His voice was cracking along with his calm, and his manic behavior seemed to expand with his theory. The occasional comment egging him on didn't help matters.

"Why's that, Sherlock?" someone asked, sarcastically.

"We're not on a first-name basis with God, and we need to be on a first-name basis. We don't have a first name for Him, so we can't be close to Him. A first name, a Christian name like Jesus."

"Jesus was a Jewish name, you dumb shit," another voice said. The critic lit a cigarette, the small amber light revealing a slight smirk on his face, accented by the red glow of the burning tobacco.

"Bullshit, man! It's Puerto Rican, like me," laughed another Marine. "And it's pronounced Hay-Zeus."

"No! No! Jesus had a first name, but God's only a last name, and we can't be on a one-to-one basis with Him if we only know His last name!"

"Is that right?" the critic said, playing along.

Why not? The rockets were still falling in and around the Company and there was nowhere else to go. It was the only show in town and at least the silly son of a bitch wasn't screaming anymore.

"His name is Frank . . ."

"What?"

"I like the name Frank. I mean, I admire it!" the theorizing Marine said, more than satisfied with his conclusion. "You can't have a one-on-one relationship with anyone unless you're on a first-name basis."

"And that's Frank?" a Marine asked, smiling in the glow of his cigarette. Oh, it was getting interesting.

"Uh-huh," the lance corporal replied. "It's a good name."

"It's also short for Francis," said the critic, while someone else smothered a laugh, "which is the name of a talking mule, you jackass!"

The Marine remained undaunted and began praying. "Please, Frank, don't let the rockets kill me! He won't. I know He won't!"

"What about the rats and snakes?"

"Not them either! Frank's will be done!" the Marine said, turning in the stagnant water, creating a sudden swell that disturbed the resigned comfort of the others in the shelter.

On a corner ledge in a three-inch passageway created by a seam in the sandbag construction, two small eyes briefly stared at the Marines, then disappeared. The animated Marine was trying to convince the others without success.

"Stop moving around so much, you asshole, or I'll break your goddamn head!"

"*Frank* damn head," laughed someone else in the dark.

Suddenly calm, and now huddling with his serene secret, the lance corporal kept up a small conversation with Frank, at times laughing and swearing, pleased with his revelation.

A few others in the underground bunker were laughing, too, but for other reasons. Among them was Sgt. J. P. Henderson, a wiry squad leader who'd heard enough to wonder if the man was drawing conclusions with a dull pencil.

"Nobody took him seriously," said Henderson, "at least not initially. Not at first. Not even when the enemy rocket and mortars stopped falling a short time after he started talking to Frank."

Henderson said it wasn't until a few other things happened that the rest of those in the bunker that evening began to wonder if maybe the lance corporal knew something they didn't! Like when he entered the mess tent one day, took his food, and said his prayers to Frank. When he had finished eating, he left the mess tent and, as he walked away, a 122mm rocket slammed into the mess tent and literally and figuratively blew it all to hell.

"Or when we'd all been flown out to the jungle for a mission, and he had spent the entire flight talking to Frank. We all exited the aircraft, and everything seemed to be fine until he stepped out. As it lifted off, it suddenly developed engine trouble and crashed in a twisted, tumbling heap further down the landing zone," Henderson said.

Then there was the jeep ride the lance corporal was taking with a few others, when he decided to walk the rest of the way because he wanted to talk to Frank. The jeep stopped and let him off, then just ten yards away, it hit a land mine.

"After that," Henderson said, "a few people began to take him and his theory a little more seriously. Stupid as it was. Personally, I thought he was just an accident waiting to happen and that his theory was just a crock! Of course, a short time later, I was hit by a 122mm rocket and almost died, while he went home without a scratch." Henderson smiled. "After that, I began thinking that Frank's not such a bad name."

NAMESAKE

S.Sgt. Deverton Carpenter Cochrane was a Ranger team leader for the 1st Air Cavalry Division's elite long-range patrol company in 1970.

During one such patrol in Cambodia, Cochrane's five-man team was ambushed at point-blank range by a North Vietnamese Army unit, and Cochrane was seriously wounded in combat and unable to escape. He is still listed officially as missing in action.

Ironically, Deverton Carpenter Cochrane was named after a relative, Deverton Carpenter, who served in the South Pacific during World War II and who, while on a long-range mission thirty years earlier, was lost in combat and listed officially as missing in action.

WE REGRET TO INFORM YOU . . .

You can't envy an officer or senior noncommissioned officer who has the unpleasant task of writing a letter informing a family how its father, brother, son, or—today—mother or daughter died in combat. Once the letter is mailed, the writer has to live with the fact that he or she has probably sent the most painful letter a family will ever receive.

This is another story in which names have been changed, told to me by someone who had that unfortunate task. His credentials and impressive military record, not to mention his job description in Vietnam, were easily verified. He prefers to remain anonymous for a variety of reasons, including his privacy and the privacy of those involved. "Even some of the idiots," he says.

> **Our duty is to believe that for which we have sufficient evidence, and to suspend our judgement when we have not.**
>
> —JOHN LUBBOCK

The job of a sergeant major (paygrade E-9) in the United States Army, in spite of what the official job description reads, is also that of a godfather, mother hen, rabbi, overseer, ombudsman, and chief shit disturber. If they don't possess the wisdom of Solomon, then they at least make it appear that they do, in starched fatigues and spit-shined boots.

As the most senior noncommissioned officer in the battalion or squadron, his scope of responsibility is far-reaching and all-encompassing. In military circles, a sergeant major is a god; maybe not *the* God but *a* god, capable of instantly calling up thunder and lightning and making the impossible possible.

Sergeants major are not merely *in* the army and Marines, they *are* the army, and the Corps; and woe to the soldier or Marine who doesn't treat the army or the Corps with the proper respect! They have been known to chew out officers whose uniforms needed pressing, soldiers of any rank whose boots needed shining, and to rant and rave over a hairline that was a fraction of an inch over what the regulations said it should be! Unlike those who heed Teddy Roosevelt's policy of speaking softly while carrying a big stick, sergeants major roar and bellow and always, *always*, with the stick well in hand, ready to strike, or lend support.

As the battalion or squadron's senior NCO, the sergeant major is also responsible for the health and welfare of the soldiers under his command and for the unpleasant jobs that go along with the position.

Sergeant Major Raymond never looked forward to paying visits to the rear area evacuation hospital. It was always a difficult task, and even after nearly twenty years in the service and two wars, for him the fighting was always easier than its aftermath, particularly the lingering effects found in the field or evacuation hospitals.

During a brief but bitter battle along the Cambodian border, four of his people had been killed in action and four seriously injured. The dead G.I.'s were body bagged, processed at Graves Registration, and then loaded into gray metal caskets to be sent home. Before the bodies arrived, telegrams would be sent out with priority, and representatives of the military units assigned the burial detail would pay a formal visit and coordinate the necessary arrangements with the families. Back in Vietnam, a memorial service would be held in the battalion area, taps would be sounded, and then the sergeant major would begin the difficult process of writing letters to the families of the soldiers he had lost.

Once that was accomplished, the sergeant major would visit the evacuation hospital. A visit, he knew, wasn't much, but it was necessary for many reasons, some of which even Sergeant Major Raymond might find difficult to define.

"To see how the boys are doing," he had explained to the colonel, unconsciously emphasizing the word *boys*. He didn't mean it in a derogatory sense; the soldiers in his command were mostly ninteen- and twenty-year-olds. They were boys, but they were also good soldiers even if no one back home seemed to think so. Even in this political mess of a war, his boys matched the best he had seen or served with.

The trouble was, this war was a political mess, a bum rap which would attach itself to those caught up in it.

The visit to the evacuation hospital, he informed the battalion commander, was just to see if the boys needed anything and maybe to make sure the "rear-area pukes" were taking proper care of them.

"Personnel," corrected the battalion commander, as he tried to fight a smile.

"Yes sir, rear-area personnel pukes. I thought I'd take along the chaplain."

"That's fine," the colonel said. For all his pomp and ceremony, gruff and hard demeanor, the sergeant major was a professional soldier who cared about his people. He was maybe a sentimentalist at heart, too, which the colonel didn't view as a character flaw, either.

"I'll be flying down tomorrow with the general to pin on a few medals," the colonel added in the awkward silence that followed. "I'd appreciate it if you would let me know if there's anything they need, will you, Sergeant Major? Anything at all."

Sergeant Major Raymond nodded and said he would do that.

Gathering up the chaplain assigned to the battalion, he flew down to the division's rear area, retrieved a jeep from a busy motor pool, and made the hot, dusty drive to the evacuation hospital. The highway was crowded with rickety buses, mopeds that sounded like small chain saws, and assorted wheeled traffic that belched clouds of blue-white smoke. The cacophony of the road, mixed with the stench of wet earth, fresh vegetation, chicken manure, and the occasional acrid smell of something decaying or burning, made the road trip in the open jeep considerably less than pleasurable.

A small bus had hit a land mine, overturned in the explosion, and blocked traffic before the wreck was eventually pushed off of the highway, along with several of its dead occupants. A wailing mother stooped over the lifeless body of a dead child drew little notice from many of the passing vehicles; the war had made an incident such as that all too common.

"I'm getting too old for this shit," he said, more to himself than to his passenger. "Let's see if there's anything we can do." He and the chaplain pulled over and started to get out, only to have a Vietnamese military policeman wave them on.

"No stop! You must go! Not safe here. Go!" the military policeman said; the sergeant major nodded, swore again under his breath, and pulled the jeep out onto the road, leaving a small churning cloud of orange dust to settle over the child.

By the time they reached the evacuation hospital, they were caked with road dust and were worn from the pounding heat of the ninety-three-degree day. As they wheeled into the hospital's parking area, the sergeant major locked the jeep's steering wheel with a heavy chain, stretched his legs, and then followed the chaplain toward the division's liaison office.

Each field hospital had liaison offices for the military units in its area, where small staffs kept the units apprised of the situations of their wounded soldiers. As it was almost noon, the division's liaison office was closed for lunch, so Sergeant Major Raymond led the chaplain to the admissions office instead. He figured he could ask to see the ward rosters to find out the status of his people. After all, you didn't just show up in front of a wounded soldier's bed and ask him when he'd be up and running only to find out both his legs had been amputated below the knee, several hours before. That was another reason for the liaison offices.

Like any business, even army business, the liaison office had its hours of operation posted while those who worked there clung to its schedule. The office had closed early for lunch, so the two travelers wandered over to an adjacent office that was still open for business.

"Good morning," the sergeant major said, opening a screen door and addressing an indifferent second lieutenant who was seated behind a waist-high office counter. Judging from the expression on the young officer's face, he was more than a little annoyed by the sudden intrusion. The clock on the wall read 11:55, which was still morning but pushing heavily on the lunch hour. Two lower-ranking enlisted personnel sat at olive drab, metal desks, watching as the lieutenant rose and walked over to the counter.

"Can I help you, Top?" asked the lieutenant.

Sergeant Major Raymond winced at the faux pas but let it ride. What the fuck? This was a friendly visit after all. No need to jump in the idiot's shit just because he didn't, obviously, know the correct senior enlisted men's ranks or titles. "Top" was the slang expression used to address first sergeants, not sergeants major.

"I'm here to see some of my people who were wounded a few days ago," Sergeant Major Raymond said, providing the unit designation and the soldiers' names. "We just came down to see how they're doing."

"Did you check with your liaison office, Top?"

"Yes, Lieutenant, I did. The office is closed."

"Then I'm sorry," the lieutenant said, taking another look at the clock. "You'll have to come back after lunch."

"Excuse me, Lieutenant?"

"It's SOP," the second lieutenant said. When all else fails, fall back on petty rules and regulations.

"Their office is closed for lunch, and we have to get back to Bien Hoa by early afternoon to get a ride back to our command. If you can help us it would be appreciated. It will only take a few minutes of your time."

"I'm sorry, but I'm afraid you'll have to wait until your liaison people return. It's SOP."

The sergeant major sighed and shook his head while the chaplain studied the height and weight chart, knowing what was coming next. He had seen it more than a few times. The sergeant major was a patient man, but patient only to a point; then the other side of the man's nature took over, in a transformation that Mr. Hyde might find frightening. "Say again, Lieutenant?"

"I'm sorry, Top. But that's the rules, and it's almost our lunchtime as well."

Sergeant Major Raymond leaned over the counter face-to-face with the young officer, only this time he wasn't smiling. He was calculating the distance. "Listen to me, Lieutenant, and listen good. Look up the names of my people and tell me which ward they're on, and while you're at it, I want you to look around to see if you can find me a big rope."

"A rope?" the second lieutenant asked, a little confused. The chaplain sighed, hearing the thunder building. Blessed are the dumb, he thought, for they, too, will be given ample opportunity to learn, even at the cost of embarrassment.

"That's right! A rope, because I'm a sergeant major in the United States Army, not a 'Top'!" Raymond said, hovering toward the young officer who was frozen like a deer caught in the headlights of an oncoming pickup truck at the counter. "And you'll need a big rope if you try to spin my ass out of here with some bullshit about me needing to see my liaison people before I can visit my wounded combat soldiers because you're worried that you'll miss your second helping of mashed potatoes and gravy or fruit cup. You understand me, Lieutenant?"

"Well, I . . ." the officer said, stammering and taken aback by the blistering barrage.

"You what? You going to march over to MAC-V headquarters and tell General Abrams that he has to wait, too? Because that's whose office I'm going to next if you try to spin me out of here with your petty bullshit excuses, especially because my combat wounded soldiers have inconvenienced you. My people didn't make an appointment to get wounded, and I don't need a fucking appointment to see how they're doing. Do you understand me, Lieutenant?"

"Yes."

"No," the sergeant major said, menacingly. "I mean, do you really understand me?"

"Yes, sir!"

"Sergeant Major."

"Yes, Sergeant Major!"

"Good. Now if you can locate the roster with my people on it and point me in the direction of their ward, I'll leave you to your lunch. It has been a long day and a miserable trip so far, and you haven't made it any better."

The flustered second lieutenant barked something to one of his two enlisted, who quickly disappeared out the door. A few minutes later, the soldier returned with the necessary information and handed it to the young officer. Judging from the smirks on the faces of the two enlisted men, they seemed to be enjoying the show. Handing the information to the sergeant major, the officer was already planning his next move. As soon as the arrogant *son of a bitch* is out of my office I'm going to the colonel's office and let him, by God, know what happened!

"Oh, sweet Jesus . . ." the sergeant major said, visibly shaken as he stared at a name on the list. Looking over his shoulder, the chaplain saw what the sergeant major was looking at and sighed heavily, turning to the young lieutenant, looking for an answer to a question that hadn't yet been asked.

Even though he had only been in country for five months, the second lieutenant had seen it before, and it always struck him odd how the grunts who sent their combat wounded to the field hospitals didn't count on any of them dying.

"It's a fact of war, the wounded sometimes die," he said, trying to take back some control. "I'm sorry," he added in a tone that was less than sincere. "We do our best, but sometimes it isn't enough."

The sergeant major's tired eyes went from the face of the young officer behind the counter and back to the roster. The muscles in his lantern jaw were taut and trembling, his face a study in concern. When he spoke, it was quietly menacing.

"I'm well aware of that, Lieutenant. This is my third tour of duty and my second war. This name here on the VSI list," he said, pointing to a name on the roster.

"VSI means he's very seriously injured, Sergeant Major."

"I understand that, too, Lieutenant, but what I don't understand is why we received a casualty report from this hospital notifying us that he had died. The wounded die, but the dead don't come back to life," the sergeant major said, suddenly cold and distant. "Two days ago, you people reported he died. I have a copy of the report that you people sent me back at my command."

"Well, obviously it was a mix-up with your liaison office, some sort of mistake. I can assure you that the soldier is very much alive and a patient on the VSI ward."

"I want to see him, just to be certain."

"I don't think that's possible. VSI means very seriously injured and . . ."

The sergeant major leaned closer. "Listen to me, Lieutenant, and listen well. I want to see him, and I want to see him now! What's more, I don't want to hear another word out of you. And not another word about you or your people doing your best, because your best isn't good enough. Just take me to the VSI ward. *Now!*" The sergeant major was in no mood to argue; he *was* in a mood to rip the head off of the pompous little prick.

Moments after he escorted the two visitors down the covered walkway that led to the VSI ward, the embarrassed lieutenant slunk away in the opposite direction, hurrying toward the commanding officer's office to report what had happened and, more important, to find support.

Minutes later, a harried hospital administrative posse entered the VSI ward and found the somber sergeant major and the chaplain quietly standing at the foot of the wounded soldier's bed. A name tag and chart identified the wounded soldier. The heavily sedated soldier's chest was rising and falling in a steady rhythm, and he was breathing through a plastic disk inserted in his throat in a deep phlegmy hiss. The left side of the soldier's face was heavily bandaged where segments of the eye, nose, and cheek had been shot away. Even sunken on the left side of his face, there was still enough of the uncovered side on the right to be recognizable. The sergeant major was embarrassed to say he hadn't known the soldier by name until he became a casualty, let alone by sight.

"What is the meaning of this, Sergeant Major?" the hospital commander bellowed. The senior enlisted man turned and faced the posse defiantly. If the colonel believed in safety in numbers—or in rank—he would soon learn otherwise.

"That's what I'd like to know, Colonel," Sergeant Major Raymond said, coldly. "We need to talk. Outside." The sergeant major turned and stormed out of the ward; a collection of confused officers and several doctors and nurses watched his sudden exit, dumbfounded, turning to the chaplain, who shrugged his response.

By the time the officer in charge stepped through the swinging door and out onto the covered walkway, the sergeant major was positioned and ready for his first assault.

"You people fucked up!" he said, more than a little angry but still managing to keep the problem in his sights.

"I beg your pardon?"

"I'm talking about the fact that you people, that is, someone here in your command informed us that the nineteen-year-old soldier in there had died!" In the cluster of gathered staff, a nurse mouthed, "My God!" and placed a hand over her mouth while another officer, a beefy-faced captain, shot her an admonishing glare.

"Well, obviously he didn't, and what's more, I don't like the tone of your voice!" The hospital commander was doing a little yelling of his own.

"Too bad, sir," said the sergeant major. "I'm not too thrilled about your a-fucking-mazing resurrection abilities or the casual way you seem to be taking this. You people reported him dead forty-eight hours ago, which means I sent out a letter to his family reporting him killed in action. Do you hear what I'm saying? *Killed in action!*"

The hospital commander immediately understood the situation. It was serious. "Well, I'm not assuming responsibility for this! It must have been a mistake and, well, quite frankly, you should be happy he's alive."

"Happy! I'm ecstatic! I can't begin to tell you just how happy I am he's still alive and not dead like you reported, more pleased than you'll ever know or realize. But that doesn't excuse the fact that ten thousand miles from here, your mistake, now our mistake, has probably killed something in his family and loved ones. Have you ever delivered the news to a family that their son or brother or father was killed in action? I have, and it's gut-wrenching. It's not like telling someone a relative has died after a complicated surgery. No, you have to go out into their wood-framed homes and ramblers and into their lives and living rooms surrounded by the soldier's baby pictures, Little League trophies, graduation or prom pictures, and tell them the worst news they'll ever hear in their lives. 'We're sorry, but your son or brother or father is never coming home again.' Oh sure, it's more diplomatic, and you apologize, and then you calmly and solemnly explain the funeral arrangements. If the strongest member of the family doesn't crumble then, well, then you tell them again how sorry you are and you leave, knowing you've ruined some part of them for the rest of their lives."

"Sergeant Major . . ." The hospital commander tried interrupting, which only caused the noncommissioned officer to continue. He was on target and firing for effect.

"Maybe at the funeral the family will accept the folded flag, or maybe they'll just stare at you, wondering if the trade is worth it."

"I understand the gravity of the situation, but—"

"Do you, Colonel? Do you indeed? Do you understand that when I leave here momentarily, I will immediately contact my battalion commander and MAC-V headquarters and see if we can somehow send an emergency telegram to his family with our apologies. *All of our apologies!* The telegram will tell them that their son is not really dead, only seriously wounded, which will wound them all over again.

"One final thing, gentlemen. You had better take good care of that soldier in there because, so help me, if I find any more of your fuckups, I'll have your asses!" The sergeant major saluted, turned without waiting for the return gesture, and left the small gathering.

"I'm not assuming responsibility for this!" the hospital commander yelled at the sergeant major's back, with no effect.

"There was no need for that," the admissions office lieutenant said, turning to the chaplain, who found himself suddenly alone in the uneasy group.

"I'm afraid there was, Lieutenant. Gentlemen," the chaplain explained, "it's not about pointing fingers or fixing blame . . ."

"It sure as hell is, Chaplain, and I understand your position," a beefy-faced captain in a crisp, freshly starched uniform chimed in in the hospital's defense. "However, our job here is difficult enough without this. Your sergeant major barges in and makes it sound as though we're inept; well, that's not the case. Mistakes happen, and you can be assured that we'll get to the bottom of this, but we will not tolerate insubordination or . . ."

The chaplain shook his head slowly, like a frustrated parent trying to get the errant child to see how he was wrong and with just as much success. "You really don't understand, do you, Captain? Colonel? Any of you? The sergeant major is a career soldier. To him, the soldiers under his command are family; maybe to you they're just patients. Maybe we're just lucky we don't have to agonize over the letters or deliver the telegrams. At times, I have trouble enough trying to keep my own faith in this mess."

"We all do, Chaplain," said the hospital commander. "But the blame in this matter—"

"You're missing the point, sir. It's not about blame. It's about grief! Grief," he said, again hoping it would sink in. "Gentlemen, I have to go." There was no pulpit there, and his preaching was falling upon closed ears. The chaplain shook his head in frustration, offered a salute without waiting for it to be returned, and then followed after the sergeant major.

During the long and difficult tour of duty as the battalion's chaplain, the captain was often surprised by what he found in the war. He had expected to find death and destruction, and in the ordeal accompanying them to learn something profound, maybe even come closer to God. He had learned that to some, words like *Duty*, *Honor*, *Country* were just words. But occasionally, he came across someone or some act that reinforced his faith and his belief in humanity.

"If you don't mind, I'd like to drive," the chaplain said, catching up with the senior noncommissioned officer at the jeep.

Sergeant Major Raymond nodded, said nothing, but moved around to the passenger's seat.

"By the way, you don't mind if I call you 'Top,' do you?"

RIPPLES AND WAVES

When you want to learn something in depth, you need to penetrate beneath its surface, but what happens when what you fear is already in the water, waiting for you?

When the dragon whispers, the wise man listens.
—CHINESE PROVERB

It's always wise to take any war story with a certain amount of skepticism, so the first time I heard about a dragon sighting in Vietnam, I was properly cynical, smug too, for that matter.

The storyteller was a retired navy chief (E-7) who had spent much of his twenty-year-plus career in Taiwan, the Philippines, and Southeast Asia. Since he hadn't begun the story with "Once upon a time . . . ," I listened a little more closely.

"Personally, I have never seen a water dragon," he said, offering up a disclaimer, before quickly adding, "However, I do know people who have, and they say they're real enough."

"Sea serpents?" I asked.

The navy veteran grinned wide and nodded. "The Chinese call them 'water dragons,' " he said. "They're not snakes, at least not from their descriptions. They're too big and ugly."

"So, were these people sober?"

The old chief smiled. "At the time they told me about them, they were. Afterward, they weren't! This was a 'bar' story, where after a few drinks, a buddy would tell you what was really on his mind. This was the kind of story that made you want to drink."

I "hmmmed" thoughtfully or thought I had faked it well enough, but he just shook his head and chuckled. Judging by his reaction, I was sure he had gotten the "hmmm" response before. "It's true! Well, at least to the people who saw them, it was."

"Okay, I'll bite. So what did these water dragons of yours look like?"

"Not mine. But what was described was thirty to forty feet long, big square head much like yours, and a two-to-three-foot-thick snakelike body, but," he said, anticipating my next question, "definitely not a snake."

"Oceangoing crocodiles, maybe?" Huge crocodiles, twenty foot and larger, had been spotted swimming miles off the coast of Australia. In fact, during World War II, there were gruesome stories of wounded G.I.'s in the Solomon Islands and Guadalcanal who were carried off by hungry crocodiles. I read somewhere, too, that in some parts of India the large crocodiles have been called "dragons."

"Naw, they know crocs when they see them. They weren't floating logs either. These had tall red plumes on their heads, tufts of something like whiskers, and snaked their way through the water before disappearing beneath the surface."

"Disappearing?"

"Faster than Jimmy Hoffa or Elvis's waistline."

"Sounds like a croc," I said.

"Dragons and sea serpents have been associated with history and lore in Western and Eastern civilizations for thousands of years. You're Scandinavian, right?"

I nodded. It was easier than saying, "Ya sure, you bet'cha."

"The Vikings had longboats that they called *drekarskips*—dragon ships—and one of the more famous ones was named *The Long Serpent*."

"Must be nice to have a library card," I said.

He smiled, called me a smart-ass, and went on with his story anyway. "You ever wonder about the dragon carvings on the bow of Viking longboats?"

"I dunno, maybe they didn't have fuzzy dice, or perhaps they wanted to scare people?" I said, remembering reading something about the sight of the dragon boats striking fear and terror into the English and Irish as they came out of the ocean's mist and into view. What did the English add to their prayers, "God deliver us from the Norsemen"?

"No fuzzy dice," he said. "But have you ever wondered where they got the model for the carving of the dragon?"

"Sagas, more than likely. Beowulf and the boys."

"That maybe, and something a lot older. They've found carvings of dragons on rocks in Northern Europe that date back to the first century."

"The first century?"

"Yeah, not to mention the English account of Saint George and the dragon," he said, bringing me along slowly.

"I thought that was just a myth from the Middle Ages!"

"Nope. Saint George was real enough," the old chief said. "He was a Roman soldier in Britain who lived in England around the year 300—"

"Three hundred?"

"Yep, and the story goes that the dragon in George's history was causing havoc in a nearby kingdom. One day, the dragon attacks a princess of the kingdom, only she's quick-minded enough to tie the dragon's mouth shut with her belt. That's when George happens along, after a busy day of booning, and slays the beast. All was right with the kingdom again, and the princess and George lived happily ever after."

"The stuff of fairy tales."

"Yep, and the stuff of history, too. As a result of that and other deeds, George became the patron saint of England. If that's not convincing enough for you, then there's always the Komodo dragon lizard in Indonesia, not to mention the frequent sightings and annual scientific search for whatever is frolicking at Loch Ness, Scotland."

"Ah, Nessie!"

"Right! And Nessie has been seen so many times, half the world believes she exists," he said. "The same thing goes for Asia. A lot of people have seen dragons in one form or another over the millennia, and swear they exist."

"Give me a for-instance, because I'm still having trouble with this," I asked.

"Okay. For instance, take the twelve signs of their zodiac. They have the rat, ox, tiger, rabbit, snake, horse, ram, monkey, rooster, dog, boar, and, guess what, the dragon! To the Western mind, they're all real creatures except for the dragon, which is a mythological creature."

"Yeah, so?"

"Yeah so the Asians believe they were or are all real. What's more, their dragons hold a lot of pull in the whole scheme of things, too. Dragons hold the highest celestial power in the Asian zodiac. The five-clawed variety came to symbolize the reign of the Golden Dragon Emperors of China, and in Taoism, there are the eight Dragon Immortals."

"They like their dragons."

"They do, indeed, and enough to believe that celestial dragons guard the gods, the spiritual dragons help mankind with wind and rain, the earth dragons guide the rivers and streams, and special dragons guard hidden treasures. They're wrapped up in every facet of Oriental life. Ours too, for that matter. Take a look at the symbol of your Vietnam occupation medal, and you'll find there's a dragon in bamboo. You ever wonder why?"

"The war dragged on."

The old chief groaned at the pun but went on anyway. "The dragon is a symbol of strength and power."

"It's an interesting premise," I said.

He laughed, knowing what I was thinking. "But you still don't think there are living and breathing dragons, water or otherwise, do you?"

"Like you, I haven't seen one," I replied. "So, beyond all the stories and myth, what do you really think?"

The chief shrugged. "I think there are things in the ocean we haven't discovered yet, and dragons may just be one of those still lurking in the depths. And then again, maybe not. However, I think too many people in too many cultures have seen *something*, and that should give us pause to think."

He was right. It was something to think about, and for several years I did. In fact, the pause lasted until 1999 when, while posting on the Internet, I came across an account of an actual, verified sighting of a dragon or sea serpent in Vietnam by Craig Thompson of Olympia, Washington.

Thompson had responded to a post I placed on a Vietnam veterans Internet discussion group about the oddest thing G.I.'s had seen during the war. Thompson said that he and others in his platoon had seen a dragon or sea serpent and offered a pretty convincing eyewitness account.

I contacted Thompson and, in an on-line interview, got his story. In Vietnam, Thompson was a twenty-year-old sergeant E-5 from Coeur d'Alene, Idaho, who was serving with Company B, 2d Battalion of the 503d Parachute Infantry Regiment, 173d Airborne Brigade.

His platoon had been bathing in the Bong Son River, Binh Dinh Province, Vietnam, when one of the Airborne soldiers spotted a large serpentlike creature swimming up the river toward the group of bathers. The creature was at least thirty feet long and one to two feet wide and was covered with golden glistening scales. Its large square head held a dark red plume that stood high out of the water as it swam, while a long undulating body trailed behind. Thompson and the others were yelling for everyone to get out of the water as they grabbed for their weapons. However, before they could react, the "sea serpent" disappeared beneath the murky waters and was gone.

The eerie sighting bothered Thompson until, decades later, he learned that what he and the others in his platoon had actually witnessed was an oarfish. The oarfish (*Regalecus glesne*) is a fifteen- to fifty-foot silver-and-blue fish with a distinct red plume on its dragon-like head, complete with long, intimidating armlike whiskers. Gold and brown variations, which also match Thompson's description, have been found in Australia and off Mexico. Some of the descriptions include a creature with a head three feet across and a mouth filled with rows of teeth, putting the oarfish very much into the dragon category.

For the doubting Thomases out there, plug in "oarfish" on any search engine on the Web, and you'll find several pictures of the creature and mentions of other sightings, including one picture taken in 1998 by Jonathan Bird when he was diving in the Bahamas. Bird took an underwater picture of the huge fish in about seventy feet of water. The picture later appeared in *Diver* magazine.

WINNING HEARTS AND MINDS

When Morley Safer of 60 Minutes *fame returned to Vietnam in 1989, the former CBS correspondent was surprised to discover that a close friend and journalist for* Time *magazine during the war, Pham Xuan An, had also been a lieutenant colonel in the Viet Cong. In his book,* Flashbacks, *Safer also wrote about Doctor Duong Quynh Hoa (pronounced* wah), *one of the sixteen founders of the National Liberation Front, who came from a prominent South Vietnamese family and was a frequent guest and friend of the American Embassy. Until 1968, when she fled to a jungle camp in Tay Ninh Province, Hoa passed along any information and intelligence she had gathered at the outings with the high-ranking Americans. What Safer discovered and perhaps confirmed was that the enemy had infiltrated almost every aspect of the day-to-day life in South Vietnam, including the visiting armies.*

David Willson, an instructor at Green River Community College, spent almost fourteen months in Vietnam. While he was not directly involved in the combat aspect of the war, he came face-to-face with the enemy almost daily. Like Safer, Willson discovered that it was seldom business. It was just personal.

Of all men's miseries the bitterest is this, to know so
much and to have control over nothing.

—HERODOTUS

BIEN HOA, OCTOBER 1967

Her name was My, but to the American clerks and
other rear-area soldiers who employed her, she was always Mamma-san, the hootch maid.

She was a small, thin, gracious woman in her midthir-
ties who maybe weighed all of eighty-five pounds but
whose lean, sinewy arms hinted of more strength than
her size implied.

She had bad teeth, decayed and blackened from a
poor diet and chewing on too many betel nuts. Though
she spoke in the same pidgin English that the other Vietnamese workers spoke, Sp5. David Willson suspected
she knew and understood more English than she let on.
There were hints from time to time.

Willson, a twenty-four-year-old stenographer clerk in
the inspector general's office, qualified for the position
in the army's legal ombudsman's office with a degree in
English from the University of Washington and by scoring high on the battery of tests the military gave to each
person entering the service.

Rank had its privileges in the military, but education
was the key to obtaining rank and a better job. Willson
had the education, and it was his education that landed
him the position. *Better,* though, was a subjective term.

In the enlisted men's hootch, Willson had seen My
locked in lengthy discussion with Deadhead Ed, another
clerk and a friend of Willson, and he wondered what
they had talked about in their animated conversations.

When Willson asked what they had discussed, the clerk just smiled.

"Everything. Nothing" was Deadhead Ed's cryptic response. "Nationalism, nihilism, and whether any system of government can really control traffic congestion, let alone hairstyles."

Willson laughed, knowing that the hootch maid wouldn't be much help, either, in solving those riddles because she only spoke in the usual French-Vietnamese-English pidgin. Except for Deadhead Ed, Mamma-san never really engaged in conversation with the other Americans.

Not that it mattered to any of the other clerks or rear-area personnel in the hootch. She was only a day worker, an invisible gook earning all of a few dollars a day in military payment certificates and whatever she could take in tips for a job well done.

"Numbah one, Mamma-san! Good job!" a specialist four said, handing the hootch maid a five-cent military payment certificate as a tip. While the nickel note might be enough for a G.I. to buy a can of beer, it was still only five cents. My had spent twenty minutes spit-shining the soldier's jungle boots to a high-gloss almost obsidian shine, and the five-cent note hardly acknowledged the effort. The five-cent note was an insult.

"You numbah ten!" My said, stalking off to her neutral corner and returning to her defined and adequately compensated household chores. Numbah ten was the slang way of saying she wasn't happy and letting the soldier know she was pissed off. Numbah one was the best; Numbah Ten was at the other end of the spectrum.

"Yeah, well if it wasn't for us, you wouldn't have a job anyway, you gook bitch!" the cheap specialist four replied as she sulked back to her work station. The G.I.

sneered, mumbled another insult, and tried to find flaw in the shine.

For the nine-to-five war-zone domestics, housekeeping made up the majority of their workday. A few women supplemented their income by doubling as hookers, but not My. She seemed content in her work, in spite of the occasional bad tip and rude remarks, sitting in that unusual Vietnamese way—a squat really—polishing boots or ironing uniforms, taking everything in and seldom giving away more than a seemingly disinterested glance.

"Hey, Willy, where you going, man?" a voice asked as Willson was heading for the barracks door. The cheap specialist four was lying on his bunk, killing time.

"In town," Willson said.

"Jesus, you still think this war is a Kodak, memorable fucking moment, don't you?"

Camera in hand, Willson shrugged. During the last thirteen months, he had learned to rely on it more than a rifle, taking carefully aimed still shots instead of hurried potshots. The rear-area soldier wanted to get a better picture of just what the war and the country were about.

Willsons had fought in the nation's wars since the American Revolution, ever since Lt. Abner Willson marched with Ethan and Ira Allen through upstate New York to take Fort Ticonderoga. But in Vietnam, that generation's representative realized there weren't any forts to take. Any military or political goal seemed muddled and badly defined, remote at best, and if we were there to save the Vietnamese from Ho Chi Minh's hordes, then the average Vietnamese citizen seemed indifferent to the process. After all, Ho Chi Minh was a hero to a majority of the Vietnamese, North and South. Commerce was booming, and the business of war, the franchising and the hustle, was everything.

During his off-duty hours, David Willson had canvassed the Saigon and Bien Hoa areas by foot or pedicab, photographing the people and street scenes. One of the more memorable outings was at the Saigon Zoo, where he offered Asian sun bears Milk Duds, taking pictures of the bears clapping for more while the Vietnamese onlookers laughed and clapped along with the small but deceptively powerful animals.

On his return, he'd rewind his film and drop off the small canisters at the post exchange for processing while picking up the pictures of the previous outings. In his footlocker, he had scores of photographs of Vietnamese, Nung Chinese of the Cholon District, the small, squat montagnards passing through and awed by so much going on around them, and the throngs of the displaced or transient people crowding the broad streets. He had pictures of the pedicabs and bicycles, oxcarts and pushcarts of the farmers and vendors going to market amidst the military traffic. He had the shopkeepers, pimps, and black-market stalls bulging with American goods, sneering street hustlers, and more.

"Got any hookers?" the specialist four had once asked over Willson's shoulder as he shuffled through the latest group of photographs.

"Yeah."

"No shit?" the specialist four said, quickly moving around Willson to get a better view of the pictures.

"Yeah. Deadhead Ed and I went through a few whorehouses a while back—in that stack," he said, tilting his head toward his open footlocker as he casually perused the new arrivals. Mamma-san shuffled over from her corner, retrieved a pair of Willson's jungle boots, glanced at the photographs without comment, and then returned to her work area.

The specialist four scooped up the pictures in the footlocker, rapidly riffling through them, only to be disappointed by what he found or, more precisely, didn't find.

"They—they have clothes on!" the specialist four complained.

Willson nodded. "Uh-huh," he said.

"Why?"

"Why what?"

"The pictures of hookers with clothes on. Why?"

"A slice of life," Willson said, knowing the specialist four wouldn't understand. He didn't bother explaining. He wasn't even sure if he really understood himself, but he knew that photography was his way of trying to make some sense out of so much that seemed senseless, as though the pictures would reveal something that maybe he and his buddies all had missed.

"Man, you gotta go home," the specialist four said, throwing the pictures back down on the footlocker in disgust and starting to walk away. "You been here too long."

"We all have, even the Vietnamese."

"What's that supposed to mean?" The specialist four said, turning back to Willson.

Willson grinned. "It means the Vietnamese took the country from the Cambodians, and maybe that's all this war is about—regionalism or, more than likely, nationalism. Theirs, not ours. So maybe we need to leave it to the people who live here to sort out their own mess."

"The Vietnamese want us here!"

Willson laughed. "Yeah, right," he said. "Like they wanted the French, the Japanese, the Chinese, and everyone else before them because maybe they needed jobs polishing boots for great tips."

"Screw you, Willson!" the specialist four said, stomping off.

"Maybe I'll extend again and screw myself," he shot

back. The target of his comments muttered something in response that Willson didn't catch.

The afternoon temperature was running into the high nineties, and David Willson, listening to the rhythmic slapping and popping of Mamma-san's busy boot-polishing rag, leaned back on his bunk, gave some thought to extending his tour of duty if only so he wouldn't have to spend any more time in the army State-side, and drifted off into a light sleep dreaming of once again being a civilian.

Twenty minutes later, Willson was startled out of his sleep when Mamma-san slammed the boots down under his cot. To his surprise, he found the Vietnamese day worker silently staring down at him. Willson sat up and said, "Yes, Mamma-san. May I help you?"

"Help yourself, Willson," she said, the pidgin English gone, replaced by a carefully precise and practiced tone.

"Willy. Call me Willy. So what are you saying?" The hootch maid smiled, but there was little humor behind the smile.

"Go home, Willy," she said. "The Viet Cong will come soon and kill everyone."

"Everyone?" Willson asked with his usual cynical nonchalance.

Mamma-san nodded solemnly.

Willson couldn't help but laugh. "Bien Hoa? This base is bigger than Rhode Island!"

"Bien Hoa, Saigon, Long Binh, everywhere. Everyone who doesn't run and hide will die. You'll see. Go home, Willy."

"So when is this supposed to happen?" Willson wasn't too concerned. It was the kind of talk that had been going around ever since he arrived in Vietnam. A day worker or cabdriver would offer the information with concern, but nothing would come of it.

"Soon."

"Soon when?"

"Soon. You go home and live and when you see the Tet fireworks on the news, you think of me, Willy." Tet was the Vietnamese New Year, which the Vietnamese celebrated with fireworks and flair, and that year's celebration was expected to be something special since the Viet Cong and North Vietnamese had agreed to a holiday truce.

"Yeah, sure. I'll go home. Why not? I'll think about you, too. Here!" Willson said, handing Mamma-san a dollar MPC note for his boots; Mamma-san waved it away.

"It isn't about money," she said. "Just go home."

On January 30, 1968, the first day of the Tet New Year, a little over two months after Sp5. David Willson had left Vietnam, the Viet Cong launched their largest and most effective offensive.

Within hours, thirty provincial capitals were savagely attacked, five of which were overrun and captured. The Viet Cong moved swiftly into seven of South Vietnam's largest cities, including Saigon.

During the surprise attack, every major American military base and airfield, including Bien Hoa, were shelled or infiltrated. The bloodiest year of the war began with a well-orchestrated, predawn signal and, perhaps, a cryptic warning from a hootch maid who wanted to spare someone she didn't consider an enemy.

AND THUNDER MAKES YOU TREMBLE

Ever hear of Joe Hooper? No? Well, you're not alone. When the Medal of Honor winner died in 1979 of a cerebral hemorrhage in a motel in Kentucky, there was little mention by the media of his passing. There was a back-page obituary in a local Seattle-area newspaper, but little else to memorialize the former resident.

Low-key and introspective, he grappled with ghosts that haunted him daily. Although he'd put away his medals and photo albums, he was never far from the distant thunder and echoes of another time. Joe Hooper deserved better than his unnoticed passing and, after you read the account of his service in Vietnam, I think you'll agree.

Show me a hero, and I will write you a tragedy.
—F. SCOTT FITZGERALD

On February 21, 1968, an Airborne infantry squad from Delta Company, 2d of the 501st, of the 101st "Screaming Eagles" Airborne Division, discovered what appeared to be the edge of yet another enemy bunker complex just outside the ancient Vietnamese imperial city of Hue.

It was just three weeks after the Tet, or New Year's, offensive, when the Viet Cong and North Vietnamese Army launched one of the largest and bloodiest campaigns of the war, and the Americans and their allies were still reeling from the volume and intensity of the well-coordinated and well-executed attacks. The paratroopers of Delta Company moved cautiously. They weren't taking any unnecessary chances.

After the imperial city had been captured by the Communists, then retaken in bitter house-to-house fighting, the Americans were making gruesome discoveries. On the outskirts of the city, in a rural tropical setting, they had found mass graves where hundreds of Vietnamese civilians had been slaughtered, dumped, and then buried by North Vietnamese execution squads. The G.I.'s curiosity overcame the putrid smell of the rotting flesh that had lingered over the burial site. Newspaper and magazine photographers recorded the recovery operations.

In the mass grave, the Americans found men, women, and children—hands tied behind their backs—shot in the head. Some had been bayoneted and bludgeoned. The unearthing also made for other, more personal atrocities as the dirt gave way to children's bodies and dead American soldiers in jungle fatigue uniforms. U.S. uniforms. The oblong gold-and-black shoulder patch identified the victims as members of the 1st Air Cavalry Division. The olive drab camouflage patch was replacing the more colorful division patch, but there were still Cav troopers who wore the original as their standard.

"We got G.I.'s here!" one of the Airborne soldiers yelled over the find as they moved more dirt. Nine Americans had also been dumped in the grave. The arms of the victims were bound at the wrist and elbow. The soldiers had been executed. White fingers clutched pumpkin-orange soil where the men had desperately tried to dig their way out. The men of the recovery crew fought to control their anger but weren't having much luck.

"You sons of bitches! You miserable sons of bitches!" one young soldier yelled to everyone and no one, barely able to control his outrage and tears, realizing what had happened to the Cav troopers. They had been bound and shot, but hadn't died before they were buried. Some of the soldiers had choked on the soil that was shoveled in after them.

Throughout the Republic of South Vietnam, the Viet Cong commandolike sapper teams and NVA infantry divisions hit many major military installations and key targets, sacrificing thousands of their soldiers in suicidal ground assaults to show that the war was far from over. In Saigon, a nineteen-man Viet Cong death squad seized the American Embassy and held a small part of the building for six hours until they were finally killed by an American assault force.

Meanwhile, in the first few days of the Vietnamese New Year, the Viet Cong and North Vietnamese Army took the cities of Hue, Dalat, Kontum, and Quang Tri and attacked major military installations throughout the country. The Communists' losses were staggering and would forever cripple the Viet Cong's effectiveness, but they weren't without their own successes either as outposts and cities fell. The tally was running over one thousand Americans killed a month, and there were larger numbers of wounded. South Vietnamese and other allied forces' casualties were significant as well. The war had taken a deadly new turn.

In the long weeks that followed, after the enemy had finally been driven from the cities, they had to be pushed out of the provinces, and that job fell to units like Delta

Company. Walking point for the Airborne infantry unit was red-haired twenty-eight-year-old S.Sgt. Joe Hooper.

Hooper, who was from the small farming community of Zillah, Washington, was a squad leader with some uncommon skills. Having grown up hunting, he was well aware of why you had to sneak up on your prey. Hooper and his people were doing a recon of a suspected enemy encampment for the company, and as they moved, their nerves were wearing thin.

They had been in contact with the enemy for one month straight, setting some kind of miserable record, and that day wasn't showing any signs of ending the string. Knowing that made the going slow. You didn't rush into an ambush unless you were stupid or had a death wish. The mission—Joe Hooper's mission—was to check out the river area in the company's area of operations. Intelligence said it showed "signs of possible enemy use."

"Signs?" someone had laughed during the briefing; the signs were everywhere.

No shit! Hooper thought, studying the much-used jungle area in his latest AO. The dropped wet-and-sticky balled rice, fresh bootprints, and pieces of equipment strewn along the trails, the sounds of someone chopping wood through the underbrush, and a Vietnamese NCO barking out a command told him more than "possible enemy use" was probable, and damn likely heavy enemy use was still in effect. The company's contact record was still intact.

It was also "possible" that the company was about to walk into a well-planned enemy ambush if it wasn't careful. The quick reconnaissance by his squad confirmed the enemy was indeed in the area, well dug-in in fortified fighting positions. They were showing no signs of leaving. What's more, these weren't Viet Cong volunteers, either, but well-armed and well-equipped North Vietnamese soldiers, hard-core little pricks who preferred to stand and fight rather than to run. Especially now.

After all, Hue held historical and emotional significance for the Vietnamese, North and South, and the NVA weren't about to lose face by abandoning it. Face meant everything in that part of the world, and especially in Vietnam, where they frequently took it on the chin to make their point. Besides, holding the cities and provinces as long as they had flaunted their resolve to the world. The offensive had been led by one of the Communists' most experienced generals, Vo Nguyen Giap. Giap was the hero of Dien Bien Phu, the tactical mind that had defeated the French, and the man who had been tasked to cripple the Saigon government, the Americans, and their allies.

Prior to the new offensive, there had been talk, in America, of seeing "the light at the end of the tunnel," meaning that the war was turning in favor of the South. But with the new offensive, the light seemed to be growing dim. The Tet offensive had demonstrated that North Vietnam wasn't about to give in. They had taken their hits, but still had come out punching at the bell.

The bout was far from over, and there were still many rounds to go. Never mind they were bantamweights against the larger, heavy hitters. It was enough to get in their licks and do as much damage in the early rounds if they were to ever go the distance. And they would go the distance. They wanted to wear the Americans down. If not the soldiers themselves, then certainly the antiwar crowd back home.

It was Ho Chi Minh who, when asked if the Vietnamese preferred to stay under French occupation or

Chinese, said "it is better to eat French shit for another ten years than Chinese shit for another thousand." Pride was everything, which was why the NVA were holding their ground; ground that the 101st Airborne was fighting to take away.

Hooper's squad had discovered a slow, mud-brown stream where freshly dug enemy fighting positions could be made out by a patient and practiced eye. Closer examination revealed a number of underground bunkers on his side of the river, too. Hooper took it all in. He didn't like the feeling the sight left with him.

"What do you think, Sarge?" one of the men with him whispered as Hooper studied the opposite bank for movement. Something didn't feel right. As they radioed in their findings and the rest of the company advanced, the NVA soldiers zeroed in on the Americans and began firing.

The heavy volume of small-arms and machine-gun fire and the *whoosh* of rockets from the rocket-propelled grenades told the G.I.'s they were facing something more than a squad or two of enemy soldiers. Hooper could hear Sgt. Clifford Sims yelling for his people to follow his lead as Sims got up and attacked the enemy position closest to him. Sims was a hard charger. That was one of the things Hooper liked about the black man. Sims wasn't the kind of NCO to sit around with his thumbs up his ass waiting to be told to do what was necessary. He took his job as a squad leader seriously. "You lead, follow, or get the hell out of the way," Sims had once said, quoting a line that summed up his own beliefs. That was all there was to it. It came with the stripes.

The volume of fire and the surprising number of positions it was coming from immediately told the Screaming Eagles that the firefight that just erupted might turn into a full-scale battle. As the Americans fired and ma-

neuvered for better ground, the incoming fire shifted
with them. Bullets and fragments of splintered projec-
tiles cut through the underbrush, tearing away branches
and limbs, filling the morning with the smell of cordite
smoke and bleeding tree sap.

There wasn't a hell of a lot Delta Company could do
unless they took out a few of the bunkers and established a foothold. Since the NVA were well dug in, any
foothold would have to be won inches at a time. The
cost of measuring the distance would be staggering.
While the rest of Delta Company scrambled to concentrate suppressive fire on the enemy line, Hooper led his
people upstream across the river and came out up on the
opposite bank to attack the nearest position with flank-
ing fire. The NVA weren't expecting an end run or
sweep, and the tactic worked. The squad overran two
positions, killing or driving out the enemy soldiers who
occupied them.

It was a toehold, at best, but Delta Company was
moving to take advantage of it. A lane had been opened,
thanks to Hooper's people. As the Airborne grunts
moved forward, they received another nasty surprise. At
first they believed that they faced perhaps a platoon of
NVA, but judging from the enemy's uniforms, firepower,
and equipment, Hooper realized it had to be a company-
size element or larger. The stakes had been raised. Delta
Company was facing well over one hundred enemy soldiers, with experienced officers and seasoned fighters.

As Delta Company pressed the attack, several soldiers
were wounded, falling in the open and crying through
the noise of the battle as they crawled, or tried to crawl,
to safety. It's surprising what carries over gunfire or what
pulls at your conscious mind during the confusion of
battle. The cries and screams of the wounded wrenched

the hearts of even the most battle-hardened veterans, and Joe Hooper wasn't immune.

The staff sergeant knew what had to be done; the medics couldn't do it all. He took a deep breath and blew it out heavily and then raced out to pull a wounded G.I. to safety. Before he reached the man, Hooper was hit in the back by enemy gunfire. He pulled up for a brief moment. The former Washington State high-school track and football star wasn't sure what had torn into him, but whatever it was had smacked against him like a baseball bat, and it burned like hell.

He cried out, swore, and then shook the wound off as he stayed on his feet and kept going. Like breaking a tackle, the impact hurt, but you still kept moving forward with the goal in mind. Besides, this wasn't a game.

When he reached the first of the two wounded soldiers, the staff sergeant managed to pull him to cover, back to safety, before returning for the second.

While Hooper was dragging the second man back to cover, a medic joined him to treat the wounded G.I.'s. The medic quickly examined Hooper, noted the wound gouged across the muscles of his back, and decided he, too, needed to be medevacked. He bandaged Hooper's wound, but Hooper refused to go.

"Take someone else," he said to the surprised medic. "I can't leave my people." The staff sergeant then returned to his squad, only to find that like the rest of the company they, too, were pinned down and trapped. The forward momentum had stopped.

To many, the situation seemed hopeless, but not to the Airborne soldier, who figured, Fuck it! and, grabbing a handful of grenades, charged the nearest bunkers by himself. With his M-16 offering just enough suppressive fire to keep the enemy's heads down and get him close enough to the opening of the first enemy position—a small one-foot-square firing port—he tossed in a grenade and then scrambled to the next enemy bunker in line, repeating the process before moving on to a third. One by one, the grenades blew behind him.

Rising black clouds of debris, swirling dirt, and an invisible wave of intense heat from the explosions followed him as he ran, the glowing splinters of metal fragments from secondary explosions tearing into his back and legs. Small holes and spreading rosettes of blood mottled his jungle fatigues. The pain spread like needles in his brain. Where the shrapnel didn't penetrate his skin, it burned red welts.

Hooper was a mess. He was covered with dirt, soot from the gunsmoke, and his and others' blood. Still charging forward, Hooper looked like a demon. The fighting was growing more hectic and confusing, and the NVA soldiers were charging out to attack, only to be cut down short of their intended targets—most of the time.

In other moments, grisly hand-to-hand combat scenes were being played out in grunting, swearing, life-and-death struggles. Sims was up to his neck in the fighting, and over the radio, Hooper heard someone say he was wounded.

Someone else was yelling over the battle, catching Hooper's attention. Hooper wasn't a medic, but he knew enough of first aid to do something to help. You stop the bleeding, apply presure, and get them to safety.

As he ran, he caught sight of two NVA soldiers who were rushing toward the battalion's chaplain, who'd been wounded trying to assist those crying for help. The chaplain was a good man, and Hooper knew it, but he was out of his element. Hooper threw himself to the ground and then crawled forward.

Hooper couldn't fire for fear of hitting the chaplain,

so just as in football, he went up the middle. But he was carrying his bayonet instead of a ball. What was the chaplain doing out there anyway? Even as he was running, Hooper knew the answer: the chaplain was there to help, doing what he could. War is hell, and the definition became clear to the wounded when the enemy closed in for the kill.

He was wounded and lying in the open; the chaplain's chances didn't look good. The enemy soldiers were almost on him, going after their prize: the American officer. Ironically, the answer to his prayer came in the form of a bloodied enlisted man.

In a running, all-out charge, Hooper yelled, drawing the two enemy soldiers' focus from the chaplain. When he was close enough, he hit them with a flying tackle, hard, plowing into them both and knocking them to the ground. In a raging fury, Hooper rose up in a tangle of arms and legs, stabbing and slashing at the Vietnamese who were trying to kill him. Moments later, the two NVA soldiers were dead, and Hooper's bayonet was bloody. Breathing hard, he helped the chaplain to cover and safety.

Once they were within a makeshift perimeter, Hooper scrambled off to shore up any holes in the shaky defense.

His adrenaline was pumping, and not knowing whether the momentum was on their side, the NCO decided it had better be. Momentum came from action, not from hiding and hoping the cavalry was coming to save them. He rounded up his people again, and they began a sweep of the immediate area, clearing three small buildings the NVA used for their own infantry support. The maneuver and new momentum gave the company a little more breathing room. After almost two hours of fighting, the battle showed no sign of letting up, which presented yet another threat.

The day was wearing down, and by nightfall, the fragile gains could easily be lost. The NVA didn't own the jungle, but they knew it well enough to take full advantage of it. They also knew the American gunships didn't fly at night, so the NVA could reclaim much of what they had given up. But all of that hinged on how much they would lose before the sun set, and that was still hours away. While the game of chess is said to simulate combat, real combat is often confusing and anything but a game. There's noise, smoke, heat, and all kinds of factors the chess experts never have to contend with. Want to play chess like combat? Fine. Give the players each a two-by-four and let them swing away at each other as they contemplate their next move.

Checkmate, hell! Grind up his pawns, napalm his rooks, gut his knights and bishops, shoot his queen in the eye at point-blank range, and then overrun the sucker while he's still deciding which way to run. Combat was seldom nice or clean.

Strategy, too, became a luxury, something for generals and other brass with field maps and planning boards, miles away from the fighting. Combat survival was always immediate and harried. Action and reaction and luck.

In Delta Company's position, there wasn't any time, and the strategy was changing with each new assault and counterattack. The fighting was getting bitter and close again.

Dead bodies lay in the twisted positions where they fell, and the wounded could be heard crawling off or being carried off, crying, leaving blood trails in their wake. Ammunition was getting low, and the firefight was turning even more desperate as resources and daylight were running out. The Americans were used to the enemy's hitting them, then breaking contact or just running when it looked as though they were losing ground. Not this time. Maybe the NVA figured they weren't losing.

Hooper swore to himself, and thinking that if only the reenlistment chief had been in when he went to reenlist in the navy, then none of this would be happening to him. He'd be on a ship somewhere or maybe in a bar on liberty, thinking about getting another tattoo like the red lips on his butt that he got in Hong Kong. "It seemed like a reasonable idea at the time," he explained to a buddy, adding that "maybe then the whole world can kiss my ass."

The navy reenlistment office had been closed for lunch, so Joe Hooper walked over to the army office and volunteered for parachute training. *Airborne!* A few months later, after basic and advanced infantry training, he found himself in the three-week Jump School program, earning his jump wings. He knew how to jump out of perfectly good airplanes and admitted after blousing his Corcoran jump boots that he looked like a real stud. Not that the ability did him much good in the jungles of Vietnam! The 101st Screaming Eagles, of World War II fame, didn't parachute this time around; very few did in Vietnam. It was mostly helicopters and, of course, jungle fighting.

Taking a quick inventory, Hooper found himself a few more grenades, giving him four, and rechecked his ammo pouches. He swore. He patted his bayonet, checking to see if it was still there in case he needed it. In basic training, drill instructors would pull out the bayonet, hold it up in front of the trainees, and ask, "What's the spirit of the bayonet?"

"To kill!" the trainees replied.

"I can't hear youuuuuuu!" the DI would yell. "I said, what's the spirit of the bayonet?"

"To kill!" they yelled again, growling. Of course, nobody really thought it would ever come to that. It was all show. All macho and testosterone and trying to convince a bunch of nineteen-year-olds they were honest-to-God badasses after all of eight weeks of training. But *this!* This was real. He'd charge them with the bayonet if it came to that, and remembering the dead G.I.'s in the mass grave, he knew he'd never surrender.

The clacking sound of the enemy gunfire erupted from a building nearby, taking his mind off the bleak thought of having to use the bayonet. In a running crouch, he scrambled to the side of the pockmarked structure but saw vague shadows moving inside. Oh Lord, how many of them were there?

With one of his four grenades, he cleared the first hootch before moving to the next in line.

Just as he reached the edge of the second structure, an NVA officer, armed with a pistol and ready to use it, came out of nowhere, but instead of firing immediately, he charged the wounded American, wanting to get close enough to make sure of his kill. When he brought the pistol up, Hooper parried the gun away, grabbing the man's arm and wrestling him to the ground, stabbing and punching at him with every ounce of energy he could muster. The smaller man with the Chinese automatic pistol couldn't find his target before the blade ripped into him. Hooper stabbed again, pushing the blade in to the hilt before ripping it up and out. There was a dull crunch, like a chicken breastbone breaking, and within seconds, the enemy officer was dead. His muscles twitched and jerked in spasms, but the man was dead. The officer slid down to his side as he moved forward.

Hooper took another of the few remaining grenades

and tossed it into the structure the NVA officer had come through moments earlier.

In the seconds before the grenade exploded, the yells and audible panic confirmed his suspicions. AK-47 gunfire sprayed the door, only to be silenced by the explosion. Bleeding, Hooper hugged the outside wall.

Protected by the building's thick base, Hooper felt a dull thud against it when the grenade went off, and breathed a sigh of relief. Inside, NVA soldiers lay sprawled in death, arms and legs askew in awkward, unnatural positions, viscera torn and steaming. Death in combat was never pretty nor easy on the stomach. Hooper began to gag, and turned away. There was no time to be sick.

Across the field, he could see others from the company taking heavy machine-gun fire from yet another building, deadly rounds tearing into the vegetation and kicking up dirt like small brown geysers. Someone from the company was yelling to the men, saying they should concentrate their fire on the building. Someone else was screaming into a radio, calling for more air support and a medevac helicopter.

Hooper was operating on fear and the adrenaline that went with it. He was so scared, he was shaking. Without thinking, he found himself running again toward that new objective, taking cover when and wherever he could find it. He was thinking, but it wasn't rational thought. If that were the case, he'd have turned around and never come back! But the company desperately needed help, and he was in a position to help—or thought he was. Somehow, even in spite of the sniper fire, he made it to the next building, then worked his way to the closest opening. The tactic had worked well enough so far, so he stayed with what he knew. This time, though, he'd

brought along his rifle. The bloodied bayonet was back
in its sheath.

Shouldering the rifle with one hand, he reached into
the pouch with the other and came out with one of the
two remaining grenades. Pulling the pin, he released the
spoon and tossed the grenade in the building, then
charged through the door seconds after it blew. Besides
the enemy soldiers killed in the explosion, he finished off
two NVA who had survived the blast. Three bursts from
Hooper's M-16 ended their defense once and for all, but
not before the bullet fragments from AK-47s bounced
off the walls and tore into the American.

The one-man assault brought additional costs. His
body was ripped with a number of serious wounds;
some he could feel but couldn't reach to treat. Worse yet,
he couldn't tell whether they were from machine-gun
rounds, shrapnel, or enemy bayonets. He had faced
them all. He was cut, scraped, bumped, and bruised. He
rested for a moment, shook the noise and pain out of his
head, and tried to figure out just what in the hell he'd do
next.

Gathering up enemy weapons and equipment, he
came out of the building. Sooner or later, he'd have to lie
down; blood loss would sap his strength until he could
no longer go on. By that time, he had four serious
wounds, wounds that bled heavily and hurt like hell, not
to mention a handful of smaller wounds to contend
with. He wrapped a field dressing around one of the
more serious wounds on his left leg and did what he
could for the others. He looked like a patchwork quilt!

Someone was screaming into a radio, calling for more
support, and Hooper thought it was a damn good idea.
Where in the fuck were they anyway? Someone had to
know the battle was going to take more than Delta
Company could offer. The NVA bastards were every-

where! Trying to outflank the Airborne soldiers, squads of NVA soldiers were driven back or killed by the Americans. It was tug-of-war combat with each side jockeying to pull the other out of the game. At times, too, it appeared as though the enemy would encircle Delta, but the grunts weren't about to let that happen.

One more time up the middle. What was that line? "Once more into the breach"? Hooper and a few others took the lead again, bounding forward, yards at a time, sometimes finding themselves way ahead of the old fighting and alone in new battles, cut off by their own advance, enemy trench lines and hidden bunkers looming out to greet them. Hooper and his people had to make the best of the situation. But the enemy was too busy to notice them or take advantage of the situation.

The Delta soldiers were fighting numerous small, pitched battles, cleaning up pockets and patches of NVA soldiers that they came across, closing with and killing them as they moved. There was no real plan to their attack, just bloody random encounters, but a clear pattern was discernible in their wake. They split up the enemy's forces and left behind dozens of bodies and an ever-widening hole that showed their direction of movement and resolve not to die.

When one small battle ended, they rested, then gathered their strength to try again. And they treated their wounded. One wounded G.I. was pleading, "I don't want to die!" as Hooper checked his wounds, then checked the man's rifle. Finding it short on ammunition, he took out a magazine of his own and locked and loaded it into the soldier's M-16.

"I don't want to die either, so cover me, huh?"

Hooper collected more grenades from other soldiers and then rechecked his own rifle. Then he pulled back the slide of the dead NVA officer's pistol, clicked off its safety, and stuffed it into the belt of his LBE. He struggled to his feet to lead yet another charge. There was nothing else he could do but keep going. There was only the next battle. Like every good soldier, he did what he needed to do to survive.

He was filthy. His face looked scarred, and it was difficult to tell the dried blood around shrapnel wounds from the black smears of gunsmoke on his cheeks and brow. His eyes burned from dripping sweat, and his body was growing weak and cold from blood loss. He would hurt later, and he would pay the price of the injuries. His body would remind him of his actions and lock the memory away to periodically remind him.

There wasn't time to be scared. But he was.

Six hours into the fighting, Delta Company was still taking fire from a final line of bunkers. Scrambling closer to get a better look at this latest problem, Hooper could see they were connected by a waist-high trench line. Enemy soldiers' helmets were bouncing back and forth between them. The NVA were reinforcing the fighting positions. The trench line was the key! Get inside it, and Delta Company could control the bunkers because the firing ports for the bunkers usually faced outward and the bunkers' openings were exposed to the trench line. That was it! The trench line!

The closer Delta Company moved on the NVA's final defense, the more intense the struggle became. By then, the battle wasn't going well for the NVA soldiers, and they knew it; they'd hold and stop the American advance or they would die. Their officers were yelling at the men, saying as much, and the volume of AK-47 fire and the *whoosh* of rocket-propelled grenades showed their desperation.

The NVA knew the trench line was their weak link

and reinforced it with more fighters. The enemy soldiers were protecting it from small single-man spider holes; holes that could not be seen until you were right up on them, by which time it just might be too late.

Joe Hooper didn't see it that way. If he could somehow get *into* the trench line and take out the one-man positions one at a time, then he'd have a running shot at the bunkers with his grenade routine.

Hooper collected all of the grenades he could find. Someone had given him an incendiary grenade, which would create one hell of a fire!

Armed and ready, he started to move out again, not having to offer a word to anybody, because by that time, they knew the script and their roles in the macabre play. To Hooper's surprise, the men got to their feet again and followed his lead one more time. Keeping up with him, though, was another matter.

The trench line! The trench line! The trench line! Hooper thought, racing to the thin channel before him under the protective fire from buddies who trailed behind unable to keep up with his pace. Pulling the pistol from his web belt, Hooper was glad he had it; it would be easier to wield, and it would be a lot more effective than the bayonet. Rolling into the trench, he kept the pistol pointed down the line, waiting for the targets he knew would appear.

Taking a slow, deep breath, Joe Hooper began his trek through the trench line, tossing grenades in any opening he saw, assuming they had to be occupied. After the first blast, two NVA soldiers crawled out of the bunker behind him. Dazed and bloody, they surrendered to the others who followed Hooper.

By this time, he had killed twenty or so NVA by himself, wounded God knew how many more, captured four maybe five others, and destroyed a whole shitload of bunkers, not to mention the buildings, and the battle still wasn't over! Tossing the last of the grenades in the openings of the bunkers he passed and rolling away from the explosions that followed, Hooper continued down the lengthy trench.

At the far end, he saw what looked like the remaining two positions in the line. His fragmentation grenades were gone, and all he had was a fucking incendiary grenade that was designed to start fires and burn through metal. There was probably nothing much inside the bunkers that would catch flame, but the grenade's searing heat would be enough at least to drive them out! It would have to do. In the distance, staccato rips of intermittent machine-gun fire and explosions from rockets and grenades spoke of a cleanup operation somewhere else.

Focusing his attention on the last remaining NVA positions, he pulled the pin on the round, red incendiary grenade, tucked the pistol away in his belt, picked up his rifle again, and turned his wrath on the final two bunkers. The incendiary grenade inside the first produced high screams and terror, and the NVA soldiers fled the position. They came out firing, only to be shot by Hooper before he moved on to the next bunker, which he attacked head-on.

There were no grenades to be had, so he reverted to his infantry training and cleared the bunker with short bursts from his rifle. Surprise counted for something, and in this case, it meant another enemy bunker destroyed.

Back the way he had come, Joe Hooper could hear a faint cry from one of his buddies, who lay twisted in the trench line. The soldier was crying for help, but it was doubtful whether a medic could make it that far up ahead of the others. Running back down the trench and picking up speed as he got closer, Hooper made it to the wounded man's side. Taking a quick glance around, he put his rifle down as he tried to assist.

In spite of how it looks in the movies, trying to help a wounded soldier back to safety while raising a rifle to fire, even an M-16, isn't easy. The rifle was out. The pistol would have to do. Besides, so far the NVA had only been a few feet away, and he hadn't had to aim very much at all!

Searching around for a bandage, Staff Sergeant Hooper caught sight of an enemy soldier climbing out of a spider hole, pushing his AK-47 out first before he hurriedly pulled himself to his feet. Before the Vietnamese soldier could raise the AK-47 and fire, Hooper brought the pistol up and felt it buck twice in his hand. The soldier fell, twisting on his side, the rifle useless in his dying hands.

Behind the dead man, sudden movement caught Hooper's attention. There was one bunker left to go. Drag-carrying his wounded buddy back to safety, Hooper turned back to the position behind the spider hole. Crawling over the dead enemy soldier, he could see the NVA fighters in the bunker moving back and forth, firing at the company. He had to take the bunker out. It wasn't a matter of choice; he couldn't carry the wounded man to safety with the enemy at his back. But he hadn't come so far only to do something foolish.

Inching closer, he saw three NVA soldiers inside, still facing out and firing at the Americans to their front. Shit! They were all officers! Hooper was close enough to see the rank insignia on their collars as he got to one knee and fired point-blank range into the position. He fired until their firing stopped. Surprisingly, he had wounded all three, breaking the back of the battle with the final assault. He could have killed them all easily but, while retrieving their weapons, decided against it.

"We've got some wounded gook officers over here!" he yelled, motioning other Airborne soldiers to his position. Then he returned to help the wounded American. "Medic!" Hooper yelled over the awkward calm. "Medic!"

Reorganizing his squad, or what was left of it, and helping the platoon and company form a perimeter, Hooper had his people check their weapons and reload their magazines. There was a lull in the fighting, but chances were good that it wasn't over. After six and a half hours, they got their first well-deserved rest, and the dog-ass-tired staff sergeant who had turned the battle almost single-handedly took his own inventory. He wasn't certain which wound hurt worse! The medics still wanted to medevac him out, but Hooper refused, saying he was still needed in the company.

"Where's Sims?" he asked a soldier he knew from his buddy's squad.

"He's dead, Sarge," the soldier said flatly, his voice hollow and tired.

"How?" Hooper asked.

The soldier shrugged. "Like you. Keeping the NVA from overrunning us." The soldier went on talking, but Hooper wasn't listening.

It wasn't until the next morning that he finally gave in. The long night had been a constant fight with the stabbing pain and nightmares of new battles, and the predawn mist had left him trembling. He hadn't slept well, if at all, and he felt like a pincushion.

Yeah, he'd go out on a Dustoff later that morning. But he was glad he had time to rest for a while and glad it was cold so that anyone watching might think that was why his hands wouldn't stop shaking.

For his actions on that day in February 1968, S.Sgt. Joe R. Hooper received the Medal of Honor. During his two tours of duty with the 101st Airborne Division in Vietnam, Hooper also earned two Silver Stars for gallantry, six Bronze Stars for heroism, eight Purple Hearts, and the coveted Combat Infantryman's Badge. He was credited with 115 enemy kills in ground combat, 22 alone on the day he earned the nation's highest award just outside the ancient imperial city. He was also cited for destroying eleven enemy bunkers and four buildings. But Hooper wasn't a "killer," even if the decorations he received pointed in that direction. Consider this: in another operation, after Delta Company had cordoned an enemy bunker complex that had been hit by artillery and air strikes, Hooper decided to try another approach.

Walking out to the middle of an open area, he carried only cigarettes and a can of C rations, thinking maybe, knowing the way they had been pounded, he could get the enemy soldiers to surrender.

A short time later, the first enemy soldier appeared and, shaking about as much as Hooper, came out to accept the cigarette. When he was convinced the American didn't want to kill them, he turned around and called his friends out to join them. Within minutes, Joe Hooper had brought in thirteen enemy soldiers without firing a shot.

"It was the greatest feeling in the world," he said later. "Nobody likes to kill people."

Years later in the Pacific Northwest, while talking to a group of students at a local community college, he said that should another war like Vietnam come about, he'd urge them all to go to Canada. But then, maybe Joe Hooper understood the cost of battle in better terms than most.

His combat decorations surpassed those of Sgt. Alvin York and Lt. Audie Murphy, two of the nation's most celebrated heroes. Hollywood made movies about each, and legends sprang up, as well. Vietnam wasn't that kind of war, and Joe Hooper died in relative obscurity.

He deserved better.

THE PREMONITION

Believe in a sixth sense? A premonitional insight to something before it happens that logic cannot adequately explain or define? There are those who do, those who say that, when it occurs, the feeling is so overwhelming and unsettling that it sends a chill through their bodies and resonates somewhere deep in their souls until they know that what they had foreseen will come to pass.

The Ranger assistant team leader believed in them, and several days before a long-range patrol behind enemy lines in Song Be, Phuoc Long Province, South Vietnam, the specialist four knew he would die on the five-day mission, and said as much.

In a series of visions and dreams, he had seen himself dying in the jungle and, in a cold, deadly serious tone, told some of his buddies. Because the nightmares were so real, frequent, and overpowering, the army Ranger reluctantly accepted his fate.

The day before the mission, the Ranger began to give away his personal possessions, saying he wouldn't need them anymore. His buddies and teammates told him that they didn't want his things and that he shouldn't be talking that way. They didn't want to hear it. It was bad luck. Nonsense too.

The soldier nodded, said nothing, and solemnly went

about giving away his personal possessions and saying his good-byes.

"He was serious, and nothing we could do would talk him out of it," said 1st Sgt. Tony Cortez, a wartime friend who had witnessed the account. "You could see that he believed it, and the odd thing was that he wasn't afraid. If anything, he accepted it."

On November 17, 1969, two days into the jungle patrol, the specialist four, the assistant team leader for a five-man, long-range reconnaissance patrol, was shot and killed by a North Vietnamese Army soldier in an exchange of gunfire, just as he predicted it would happen.

CHOW

Cultural differences became apparent to even the most casual observer in Southeast Asia, but then, things weren't always what they seemed. Here's a lesson from a veteran who was hungry for knowledge and, of course, dinner.

Just outside Camp Gorvad, the 1st Cavalry Division's forward base camp, in the dusty colonial plantation village of Phuoc Vinh, the two infantrymen decided to get something to eat.

The soldiers had been in the village most of the morning, and as it was a little past noon, they knew they couldn't make it back to their mess hall in time for chow.

There were small bars that offered snacks of one kind or another, but one of them wanted something more substantial, so they settled on a small outdoor café.

The open-air café was little more than a handful of wooden tables and mismatched chairs spread out over an uneven concrete slab. It was a rustic setting, and the well-worn and weathered checkered tablecloths, the small glass vases holding mismatched, wilting flowers, implied the faded ambience of a time long since gone.

An old Vietnamese man, dressed in a tattered French-cut jacket, led the two Americans to one of the tables and handed them a handwritten menu in French and English.

A small shack surrounded a crude kitchen where an old woman with a bamboo whisk worked an oiled wok over an open-flame stove. A sizzling hiss implied something was cooking, and the spicy aroma overcame any hesitation in their decision to enter.

There were few main courses on the menu, and most were Vietnamese noodle, *pho*, dishes. The drinks available were beer, wine, and cola. The specialist four ordered beef with noodles and a 33 beer. The sergeant passed on the food and only ordered a beer. When the order arrived, it was in a small blue and white Chinese ceramic tureen. The garlic, onion, and Vietnamese spices from the *pho* offered up an aroma that the spec four found pleasing enough as he lifted a spoonful of noodles and meat for closer inspection. The spec four took a cautious bite, nodded, and then abandoned any concern as he ate with glee.

When he had eaten much of what was in the bowl, he looked up to find the sergeant smiling at him.

"So, what are you eating?"

"Beef noodle soup, sort of."

"So, you think that's really beef?" asked the sergeant, leaning back in his chair and crossing his arms.

The spec four shrugged. "Water buffalo, maybe," he replied, taking another bite. Although he hadn't seen a cow anywhere in Vietnam, every village had a few working water buffalo.

"You really think they'd use one of their natural tractors to make you your quarter pounder?"

"What do you mean?"

"I mean, I doubt if what you're eating's ever been at home on any range, Sparky."

He had a point, and the spec four knew it. In the rural

countryside, there were never more than a few water buffalo to be seen, certainly not a herd, nor had he ever seen the Vietnamese butchering one, either. He lowered the ceramic spoon and studied his bowl with suspicion. "What kinda meat you think it is?"

"I dunno. Let's ask." The sergeant called the waiter over and in broken French and pidgin English made the inquiry. When the answer came, the sergeant's smile grew wider.

"*Chien*," he said.

"What's *chien*?"

"It's dog."

"Dog?"

"You got it," said the sergeant. "So, when you're done, do you want to chase a jeep back to camp or something?"

COSMIC JUSTICE

*The official seven-day leaves for G.I.'s away from the
Vietnam War were better known as R & Rs—rest and
recreation. The escapes were designed to help relieve the
stress associated with combat by providing free flights to
such exotic locations as Hong Kong, Taiwan, Tokyo,
Hawaii, Australia, and Bangkok. All the G.I.'s had to
provide was enough money to pay for the seven days'
room and board, which was easy enough to do for many
who were caught up in combat because there wasn't anything to spend their pay on in the jungle or at the small
bases they lived on anyway. It wasn't uncommon for the
G.I.'s to spend three to four months' combat pay in the
week, and then three to four months afterward smiling,
but not always for the obvious reasons!*

Lord grant me chastity—but not yet.
—SAINT AUGUSTINE

It was a seven-day R & R away from the war zone.
One full week of rest and recreation in Bangkok, Thailand, and for the two army LRRP/Rangers, it was an opportunity to get a firsthand understanding of Bangkok's
much sought after carnal pleasures. Sightseeing didn't
outweigh the distinct possibility that, with wallets filled

with money, they'd have more than a fair chance at getting laid.

Like the good long-range reconnaissance soldiers they were, long before they arrived, they knew they could find what they were looking for in the Orient's leading sin city.

What's more, they had not only heard *all* the stories but even knew a few by heart. Like the legendary "basket trick" or the stripper who could do interesting things with Ping-Pong balls or the two female "health technicians" at one of the many steam baths who'd lather your body with scented soap and then scrub you up and down with their naked bodies, and many other real and imagined pleasures.

When they arrived at the Camp Alpha R & R processing center adjacent to Tan Son Nhut airport, their enthusiasm was more than bubbling over, like kids at Christmas, anticipating the toys but burdened by the long wait getting to them.

Dressed in their jungle fatigues, spit-polished jungle boots, and black Ranger berets tilted at the precise don't-give-a-shit angle, they'd purchase new civilian clothes in Thailand to supplement the few articles of civilian clothing they'd brought with them from the World or bought at the PX the week before. "Not that you'll need a great deal of clothing," they had been told by their buddies, who had already visited the Thai city.

The two LRRP/Rangers were ready and, judging by the expression on the faces of the others at the R & R Center, they weren't alone.

"You soldiers going on R & R?" asked a sergeant first class who was also standing in line at the center office. Already in his late thirties, his thinning black hair was showing signs of gray, which he discovered would appear darker if he slicked it back with Brylcreem. His khaki uniform displayed two rows of ribbons that said he wasn't a combat soldier but that he was a lifer.

Most conspicuously absent was the Combat Infantryman's Badge or any other combat ribbon or award that said what his job was in Vietnam. One of the two LRPPs, a short, stocky, street-wise, black New Yorker, didn't recognize the collar brass but correctly guessed it to be the administrative branch.

"You bet, Sarge. What about you?" the second of the two LRRPs replied. He was a tall, thin towhead with sharp features, deep-set green eyes, and a distinct cowboy drawl.

"I am, but you're not. At least, not like that, I hope!" said the sergeant first class, drawing the attention of another senior NCO who worked at the center. "You're out of uniform. Those berets are unauthorized."

Shit! thought the black LRRP. Here we go again!

"The berets are authorized for 75th Ranger companies . . ." offered the New Yorker, knowing the drill. In the army in Vietnam, it was the Regular Army types who wanted to steal thunder from the Rangers and diminish their importance or accomplishments by reminding them that their cocky, elitist, we're-better-than-you-are attitudes didn't carry much water or weight in the rear areas.

The LRRP/Rangers viewed such RA lifers as fuckheads who were too afraid to do the real job of the army. After all, the Ranger companies were volunteer and open to anyone who had the balls to go behind the enemy lines in five- or six-man teams and screw with Charlie or the North Vietnamese Army. They were cocky, but they had to be. The job demanded confidence as well as the need to be better than the other guy, especially the Viet Cong or NVA soldiers. Meanwhile, the sergeant first class was thinking of them as prima fucking donnas. He'd put them in their place.

Such skirmishes were part of a running battle that lasted the length of the war, and the two LRRP/Rangers and the opposing sergeant first class were just locked in another of its petty little battles.

"They're authorized in country, Sergeant. You're leaving Vietnam," the sergeant first class reminded him. "Even if it's only for seven days. Now, if you don't have the appropriate headgear for the trip, then maybe you'll want to find a clothing sales store and purchase one. But I can assure you, you're not getting on the plane dressed like that! Isn't that right, Sergeant?" he said to the noncommissioned officer at the center, looking for the support he knew he'd find. The other senior NCO wasn't sure, but if the sergeant first class was so certain, then it must be so!

"That's . . . eh, right," the center NCO said.

"What are you busting our chops for?" the towhead cowboy asked the sergeant first class, getting a little heated under the collar, not really giving a damn about the NCO's rank or status.

"At ease!" the sergeant first class barked while the New Yorker calmed down his buddy and led him out the door. Inside he could hear the sergeant first class laughing along with the second senior NCO working at the center.

"Who the hell he think he is?" asked the cowboy, still steaming from the encounter.

The New Yorker thought it over and offered his assessment. "He's an asshole who don't like us and who'll keep us from going on R & R or maybe help us miss our plane if we don't play his fucking game."

The stocky sergeant was right, and the second man knew it.

"Yeah, but it's our *berets*, man!"

"Yeah, but it's seven days in Bangkok. We say 'Fuck

him,' and we don't get laid. You hear what I'm saying?
No R & R!"

The cowboy mulled it over, then nodded dejectedly.
"Yeah, I understand," he said finally.

"Good. Then let's go find the PX," the New Yorker
said. The two men's hopes weren't about to be damp-
ened by the arrogant prick. After locating the base exchange, they bought the official baseball-type caps, and
then returned to the center for processing. Later that afternoon, they boarded a Boeing 727 for Bangkok and
tried to forget the incident. The son of a bitch sergeant
first class was up in front, and they were well to the rear
of the plane, and all was right with the world.

Once in Thailand, after the customary briefing on dos
and don'ts, the two LRRP/Rangers found a hotel, show-
ered, and then hurriedly changed into odd civilian
clothes that belonged to other neighborhoods and ethnic
settings. The New Yorker had a tailored one-piece forest
green jumpsuit and expensive Italian shoes; the cowboy
was dressed in jeans, well-worn cowboy boots, and a
T-shirt.

When they decided they were ready, they caught a cab
and told the driver to take them to Patpong. "To hell in
a handbasket, if you please," the cowboy said, grinning.

"There it is!" the New Yorker said, thinking that
maybe seven days might not be enough. The infamous
heart of sin city was about to prove that Dante was
wrong. Patpong was its own level of hell, but what
burned there were desires based on lust, greed, and other
Western notions that most Thais working the district
found humorous or just part of the human condition.
The Thais, like many Asian cultures, knew that sexual
desire was a natural part of life and was no more a sin
than feeling hunger and taking care of the need. In Pat-

pong, with only a little looking, they'd find a new level of the netherworld they were searching for, complete with blaring rock and roll, country and western, Motown soul, and the hustling pimps and giggling bar girls, mixed with the pungent smell of marijuana that wafted through the busy streets where everybody came to play or work or work at playing. Sex in Bangkok was a thriving business. The streets were alive with G.I.'s and Japanese businessmen and hawkers trying to pull people into open-door clubs, each blaring a different kind of music.

Small, lithe, long-haired Thai girls with big brown eyes and dazzling smiles worked with the hawkers or hustled on their own to drum up business.

The two soldiers had saved enough pay for the seven days of their vacation, and their fantasies had had months in the humid jungles of Vietnam to blossom. To be on the safe side, they paid for their hotel rooms in advance, as they had been told to do by their buddies back in Vietnam, who had visited Bangkok and were eager to share their R & R experiences and knowledge. "That way you'll know exactly what you'll have left to get fucked up on!" they all had said knowingly. R & Rs were more than vacations; they were shared experiences, bold, ribald tales that brought grins and smiles for a thousand and one nights or more.

"See, Bangkok's the only city in the world named after it's number one activity! You can get screwed, blued, and tattooed there and, if you're conscious, enjoy every minute of it! Hell, even if you're not, you'll still wake up with a smile on your face. There are massage parlors where you'll walk in, sit in a chair, while smiling, good-looking women are paraded before you in short dresses for your selection—"

"What do you mean selection?"

"Just that, cowboy. Each of the women have numbers

pinned to their dresses. You just pick the one or ones you want, mix and match and do all kinds of algebra, and not only will you know what X is, you'll qualify for MI fucking T."

"What's MIT?" the cowboy asked, knowing it had to be something erotic; something dirty by the way it sounded.

"It's a fucking school!" the storyteller explained, somewhat annoyed.

Cowboy smiled, picturing it as just that. "Aw-right," he said. People often mistook his accent and ways for those of a Texan, only to hear him say, "Oklahoman, which is kinda like a Texan, only we don't marry our sisters or shit in our boots!"

There was no confusing the New Yorker's accent or attitude. He used the word *fuck* as a verb, in staccato-crisp remarks. In Harlem you either became very smart at surviving or stupid enough to go to jail more than once, or worse. The New Yorker was a survivor. The army was his out and the Rangers his direction for his pride. He was a "black," which really meant he was toffee brown, but *black* was then the in-word since *Negro* had gone out of favor.

While he was suspicious of damn near all whites, talk-nice liberal or otherwise, he had learned to trust and rely on a few on his team and in the long-range patrol company, and maybe even a few others in the army. Sure, some were motherfuckers, like the rear-area sergeant first class, who probably thought of him as a "nigger" and would never come to understand any aspect of what it was like to be a LRRP/Ranger, let alone a black. But there were others, like the cowboy, who became friends, real friends, and not the bullshit army-buddy kind. *Buddy* sounded too much like that Mr. Rogers shit and what they had was something more. The New Yorker wasn't without his own prejudices, either, thinking no-good, dumb honky motherfucker on occasion only to prove himself wrong or right in the assumption. The trouble was a good stereotype never held true. It would be easy to hate if every one of "them" was a shithead, only they weren't. One of "them" was always ruining it by being nice or decent or good or caring or willing to risk his life to save yours. The no-good, dumb honky motherfucker.

Combat had made the LRRP/Rangers friends, forcing them into a bond they would only begin to understand years later. Just then, they were team members and partners in smiling R & R conspiracies. After the cabdriver dropped them off on the edge of Patpong, they wandered the streets with no other plan than desire, which meant they were very soon to engage in their first round of sinning!

"You like?" a small woman said from an open doorway, pulling the top of her blouse down and showing the New Yorker two small but well-formed breasts. Long black hair fell to the center of her slender shoulders. Licking a finger, she ran it over the taut nipple of her right breast and brought it back up to her lips. "Mmmm," she said, pursing her lips together. "Sucky-fucky, twenty dollar."

"Say what?" The New Yorker's brown eyes were riveted on her breasts. The cowboy's mouth dropped open in startled fascination.

"You and your fren, I sucky-fucky, twenty dollar." The New Yorker looked at the cowboy, and both laughed. The woman gave up on the G.I.'s and began to work a group of Japanese businessmen who were wandering the streets.

"I think I'm going to like this town," the cowboy said with a grin. "I think I'm going to like this town a lot!"

"No shit," the New Yorker said. "You know we're going to get the clap, don't you?"

"I hope so," replied the cowboy. "Doc said he's got all the pills we'll need to cure it lined up, ready and waiting when we get back." "Doc" was the platoon's medic, who seemed to spend a lot of time passing out antibiotics to G.I.'s returning from R & R and lecturing them on the wages of sin. Of course, he kept copious notes so he'd know where to go on R & R when his time came.

"Fuck our way to exhaustion!"

"'Til our balls explode!"

"There it is!"

The New Yorker led the cowboy into a dimly lighted bar where three topless women danced on three separate, well-lighted stages to something by Credence Clearwater, later turned into a real smoker by Tina Turner. The dancers were bathed in glaring red and yellow lights and mouthing lyrics they didn't really understand about steamboats on a river but gyrating to them seductively anyway.

An L-shaped bar manned by an army of bartenders wearing starched, white, short-sleeve shirts and black bow ties carried out orders to the line of American servicemen who watched the show with amusement while buying drinks for the two and three giggling women who joined each of them at the bar and sometimes, seemingly, at the hip. At booths that ringed the bar, another army of nicely dressed hostesses groped G.I.'s or eyed new arrivals like the New Yorker and the cowboy, who were doing a little eyeing of their own.

A rope separated a small section of the bar where a few middle-aged Western businessmen were having quiet drinks with one-on-one hostesses who didn't seem to be part of the general offering. When the two soldiers walked toward that section, a table of hostesses sitting in a back booth caught their attention and waved them over.

"No! No! *Here!* You come *here*!" they said, giggling and urging the two Americans over.

What the hell, the New Yorker thought, the women over there weren't any prettier than these ladies and there weren't that many in the roped-off section anyway.

"Hey baby," the New Yorker said to one of the two Thai women closest to him. Large, brown, liquid eyes flashed as she smiled.

" 'Hey baby' yourself," she said. Then, in Thai, she told some of the other ladies at the table to leave. After all, it was business.

"Please join us," a second woman said to the cowboy. It wasn't her brown eyes that attracted him to her initially, it was her large breasts and low-cut blouse. The cowboy had never seen an Oriental woman with such large breasts before, and his look said as much. "You a bar girl, yes?"

"I am a hostess," the woman replied.

"Yeah, well, nice cupcakes!" he said, eyes locked onto the woman's breasts.

"You sit here," the large-breasted woman said, scooting over and making room in the dimly lighted booth for the cowboy, who obediently said "Yes, ma'am!" and took the seat. The New Yorker slid in next to the other hostess. The seats were black plastic made to look like leather, and the table was large enough to seat a squad of soldiers or at least a baseball team. On the white linen tablecloth, the women's drinks looked low and ready for a refill.

"You buy me drink?" the liquid-eyed woman asked the New Yorker, who nodded. The cowboy followed his lead. "Damn straight!" he said.

The New Yorker ordered a round of "teas" for the

two women and two mixed drinks for himself and the cowboy. The games were to begin.

An hour or so later, the son-of-a-bitch sergeant first class, dressed in a tan safari suit, entered the bar and started toward the back booths when his eyes finally adjusted to the dim light. James Bond with a slight paunch and a license to kill time. He recognized the two Rangers but said nothing. But he stopped short and veered away, pretending he didn't see them. He turned toward the roped-off section without acknowledging their presence. Slowly removing a filtered cigarette from a gold cigarette case, he tapped it twice, the way he had seen Sean Connery do in the movies, before placing it in his mouth. A silver Zippo brought a flame to the cigarette, ending the small show. The epitome of suave, or at least he thought so.

"Hey look! It's Double-O E-7!" the cowboy yelled, while the New Yorker laughed at the greeting.

The sergeant first class ignored the comment. At least, he pretended not to hear it. In Thailand the two LRRPs didn't give a rat's ass about what authority he might think he had. Several of the other hostesses seated in booths adjacent to the two LRRP/Rangers were trying to get his attention, but he wasn't having any of it. His focus was on the roped-off section and a tall, thin woman who was sipping a mixed drink and looking coy. That was only part of it. The rest was proximity, and they knew it.

"Guess we're not good enough for him, huh?" the cowboy asked.

The New Yorker snorted. "He thinks his shit don't stink."

"No big thing. One of these days, cosmic justice will get him. It don't mean nothing!" he added loud enough for the sergeant first class to hear, then the cowboy turned his attention back to more important issues at hand or soon to be.

"Cosmic what?"

"Justice, man. Justice. You fuck with the universe or any of the good vibes in it and zap! It gets even. He had me hot back in country, but the more I thought about it, the more I knew that it'll all come back to him. Life's a wheel, man. Everything comes back to us in one way or another. Cosmic justice is what it is."

The New Yorker stared at him for a moment to make sure he wasn't pulling his leg. "You believe that shit, don't you?"

The cowboy nodded.

"Your fren on R & R with you?" the liquid-eyed woman said, asking the obvious as she slid her hand up the New Yorker's thigh and began a slow, stroking gesture. The hair on the back of his head stood up. Of course, that wasn't all that was rising either.

"Uh-huh," he said. "But he ain't no 'fren.'"

The sergeant first class said something to the coy hostess, who nodded, then moved over to let him in. The sergeant first class settled into a small table in the roped-off section and was joined immediately by another of the "special" hostesses, who glowed behind the orange spread of light from the cigarette she was smoking. Tall and slender, her movements were graceful, but calculating, her shoulder-length, shiny black hair well coiffed and stylish. The sergeant first class ran a hand over his slicked-back receding hair and smiled back toward the two Rangers. All's fair in love and war.

"He not like you, I think."

The New Yorker smiled and shrugged. "No," he said. "He's not like us at all." From time to time, the New Yorker glanced in the motherfucker's direction and saw that he seemed to prefer the special attention he was receiving in the special area. By the way he tossed around his money and by the extravagant tips he was providing to the waitress, the drinks were probably more expensive there.

Big spender! the New Yorker thought. And the man thinks *we're* elitist? No rednecks or niggers there, the New Yorker thought before he turned away to watch the entertainment on the raised stages. Several of the dancers were very good, and besides the obvious erotic qualities of their movements, they'd obviously been trained in dance. Tina Turner would've been proud; Ike would've been drooling!

"You looking for all-night girl?" the liquid-eyed Thai woman asked, getting back to business.

The New Yorker said yes again.

"Un-uh," she said, moving her hand up to his penis and letting it rest there. "I think you found her."

"I think so, too."

"You like?" the large-breasted woman asked the cowboy, who couldn't take his eyes off of her blouse. His grin expanded considerably.

"I'll say."

"You want to?"

"What?"

"I say, you want to?"

The cowboy looked at the New Yorker, who laughed and gestured "Go ahead" with his hands while the liquid-eyed woman won back his attention by flicking her thumb and forefinger lightly against the head of his now erect member.

"Fifty dollar," the large-breasted woman said, pulling her dress down a little and exposing large, brown nipples.

"Fifty dollar!" the cowboy was shocked. That seemed pretty damn high.

"Yes," laughed the large-breasted woman, pulling his face into her breasts only to have the cowboy nuzzle and kiss the perfumed flesh. "Good price. All night long. You like."

"I don't know . . ."

"Dunno what?" she said, straightening up and pulling her dress back into place. The sampling was over. The test drive completed. Now she'd either close the deal or send the cowboy off to another dealer to kick the tires and haggle. Time is money in any language or culture.

"I don't know if I can all night long," he said, draping a hand back over her shoulder and resting the heel of his palm on the rising swell of her chest. He fingered her warm nipple as his heart beat an ancient rhythm in his loins. His brain had been out of the bargaining mode five seconds after he entered the bar. "But fifty dollars is fine."

The large-breasted woman smiled again. "Oh, you will," she said, holding out her hand as the cowboy reached into his wallet, retrieved the money, and handed it over to her.

"You have hotel room?" she asked, tucking the fifty dollars away in her dress.

The cowboy nodded.

"Then, we go," she said matter-of-factly and, turning to the other woman with the liquid brown eyes, said something in Thai. Girl talk or, perhaps, strategy. Both giggled, and a small thin hand covered the mouth of the Thai hostess seated next to the New Yorker.

The big-breasted woman motioned over a third woman standing at the bar, who straightened her short red dress as she walked over and grabbed the cowboy's other arm. Placing it around her shoulders, she leaned up and kissed his neck. Her tongue flicked lightly over the skin and sent a chill through his spine. The third woman was cute, with a round face with delicate features, but not as well endowed.

"Hey! What's going on?" he asked, while the large-breasted woman eased her arm around his lower back and the two women started walking him toward the door.

"You say to. Now you don't want to?"

"Oh, you meant *two*," the cowboy said, realizing his sudden windfall and nodding in understanding. "Two!" he said again, this time to the New Yorker, who was laughing at the cowboy's good fortune.

"Sure. You no unnerstan English?"

"Hell! I think I'm just beginning to understand Thai! You okay, man?" he said to the New Yorker, who nodded.

"See you tomorrow, Cowboy!" the New Yorker said as he turned his attention back to his own hostess. Contracts were still being negotiated, but the deal was done.

"Yee-haw," he laughed.

"Your fren Yeehaw?"

"No, but he will be."

The liquid-eyed woman didn't understand, but she laughed anyway.

"You want two girls?" she asked. The New Yorker shook his head.

"No. Just you tonight," he said. She smelled of jasmine and made the young sergeant think of someone else back home, but only for a moment. There was no sense dwelling in the past while the present was smiling in front of you.

"Twenty-five dollar," she said. "But you tip me if you think I'm good."

"No problem," he said, handing her the money. In the roped-off section the sergeant first class was doing a little bargaining of his own with his professionally coy hostess and the second woman. With the offer accepted, he was being led in the direction of a small room in the back for more immediate attention. He brushed slicked-back hair again and shot the New Yorker a haughty look, which he missed because the New Yorker's attention was locked on the liquid eyes of his own hostess.

"You like. I promise. You like very much. We finish drinks and then we go to my place," the liquid-eyed woman said.

"Not the back room?" the New Yorker asked, motioning toward the sergeant first class, who smirked and then headed toward the door with his date. "Like him?"

The hostess looked at him questioningly. "You want *katoy*?" she asked.

"What?"

"I say, you want *katoy*? You know, *boy*?"

The New Yorker was outraged that she'd even suggest such a thing. "Are you crazy?"

"Not me! You the one point to *katoy* sucky room!" she said, pointing to the roped-off section.

"What?" The New Yorker was genuinely surprised for a second time. A small smile began to form at his lips. "You mean . . ."

The Thai woman nodded. "He boy dressed like girl. *Katoy*."

The New Yorker was laughing loudly now, and then suddenly became very quiet. "*You're* a woman, aren't you?"

The Thai woman stared at him strangely. "Of course!" she said, taking his hand and placing it beneath her skirt for verification.

The New Yorker laughed again. "Yeah, you're a woman, all right!" So the arrogant sergeant first class was going into the sucky room with a boy dressed as a girl, and he didn't even know it. What did she call it, a *katoy*-toy?

"Don't forget to moan, 'Oooh baby!' Sarge!" he yelled across the bar. The sergeant first class ignored him and followed the *katoy* into the back room.

The LRRP/Ranger laughed at the situation. The cowboy was right! There is cosmic justice after all! He couldn't wait to tell the cowboy and maybe tell the sergeant first class, too, when they got back in country and retrieved their black berets. Something subtle like: "Hey, Sarge, you know what a *katoy* is? Why don't you take your fat ass and find out?" and leave it at that. The New Yorker broke into a deep, sustained laugh, thinking about how he would do it.

"We go now," his hostess said matter-of-factly. She started to rise, but the New Yorker pulled her gently back down.

"Uh, not yet. I can't. You've, eh, made an impression," he said, motioning to his lap, where his erection was clearly evident. He leaned back in the booth, spread his hands as if to say there's not much I can do about it, and shrugged.

The liquid-eyed woman giggled. "Oh!" she said, understanding. "I better than *katoy*. You see!" She leaned over, stuck her head beneath the table. Her hands were busy and deft. The New Yorker started to protest, only to have her reappear and take something out of her purse.

"Ginger," she said, smiling as she disappeared once more back beneath the table. On stage the topless dancers were moving to the Rolling Stones, who were singing they couldn't get no satisfaction. The New Yorker realized Mick and the boys had probably never been to Bangkok.

CHERRY BOY

In combat, a soldier, sailor, airman, or Marine soon learns his strengths and weaknesses; it is what he learns afterward that helps him shape his path. Here is another R & R story of a group of Marines on leave in the Philippines, and of one Marine's battle to fit in.

Nineteen years of age, the Marine rifleman looked three to four years younger. He was small, thin-boned, and his 120-pound frame gave him the size and look of someone hoping to make the junior varsity track team.

Of the group of Marines on R & R in Manila, the Philippines, he was the only one who looked sorely out of place in the bustling dance bar, but he was definitely in the running for a good time. He and his buddies were on the third day of a seven-day R & R, and they were in the third dance club they had visited in as many nights.

The barker who had pulled them in led them beyond a no-nonsense fireplug of a bouncer and through the door that opened to reveal the objects of their most wanton desires. Dozens of scantily clad women were dancing with American servicemen or sitting with them at small booths or tables, talking, drinking, laughing, and professionally planning the evening's sin.

On an elevated stage above the dance floor, a disc jockey played requests the G.I.'s handed him on slips of paper, with an accompanying tip. Twin column speakers pulsed from the cranked-up volume. The Americans seated at tables close to the speakers couldn't even hear the lies the women were telling them while rubbing their thighs.

Three bartenders stayed busy behind a well-stocked bar. A second bouncer sat on a stool next to a beaded doorway and stairwell.

"You see, friendly hostesses!" the barker promised the smiling Marines. "And a stairway to heaven!"

"Think we'll get laid here?" asked one of the Marines while another surveyed the surroundings. There had to be two women for every man in the bar.

"Oh yeah!" said another, watching as the barker waved over a group of Filipinas, who hurried over to greet the new patrons. The dim light of the dance bar was kind to several of the older hostesses, and it enhanced the physical charms of the younger ones. Bright eyes, practiced smiles, and faux jewelry glistened, and if the short, tight, low-cut dresses and waves of perfume hadn't overwhelmed their senses, the Marines were nevertheless lost when the women sidled up to them, tucked their arms around their waists, and pressed their breasts and thighs into the giddy guests.

"Here is good," laughed the first Marine. "Here is definitely good!"

Pairing up with the newly arrived patrons, the hostesses led them to several empty tables where they would divide and conquer their partying prey. Drinks were ordered, quickly dispatched, and then reordered.

"You *baby*!" said one of the smiling ladies, brushing the close-cropped buzz-cut head of the young-looking rifleman, who smiled awkwardly and blushed at the remark.

"He's a cherry boy!" yelled one of his buddies, a 60 gunner. "This is his first time!"

A "cherry boy" was a virgin, and several of the ladies at both tables were enjoying the young rifleman's obvious discomfort. They squealed with delight and moved in to surround him. When they left their Marines, other women quickly moved in to take their places. As drinks were ordered and delivered, several of the hostesses dragged two Marines up to dance, while the machine gunner, the cherry boy, and four hostesses remained seated at the table.

"So, how much to get him his first time?" asked the machine gunner as two of the four ladies giggled at the thought of breaking him in.

"First time twenty dollars!" laughed one hostess. Another of the girls shook her head and lowered the price to fifteen dollars.

"No! *No* charge for first time," said the oldest of the four ladies. She was sitting in the young rifleman's lap. "He's mine!"

"No, he's mine!" said one of the younger hostesses hugging the young Marine. But the argument was quickly settled by the lap sitter. "I think I win," she said, wriggling in his lap and sensing the reaction she'd sought.

The cherry boy was beyond shame, and his eyes and smile were huge.

"Make it good!" The machine gunner laughed.

"It's always good, but for him, I make it better!" the lap sitter said, getting to her feet, pulling the young rifleman up behind her, and leading him away to a stairway guarded by yet another bouncer.

"Hoo! Hoo! Hoo!" barked the machine gunner, and the other Marines on the dance floor joined in the chant until the young rifleman pushed beyond the beaded curtain and disappeared up the stairs.

While many had watched him go up the stairs, few had noticed his triumphant return. They were involved in their own bidding wars. The hostesses who were at his table were on the dance floor waving him over. "In a minute!" he said, walking back to the table.

"Look what I got!" said the young rifleman to the 60 gunner. In his hand, he was carrying a pair of black lace underwear.

"Souvenir?" asked the 60 gunner. The young rifleman smiled and nodded.

"*All right!*" said the 60 gunner, ordering another round of drinks as he told his hostess to reserve a room for later. He reached in his wallet and handed her the money. After she had gone, he turned back to the cherry boy. "So, how many does that make?"

Pocketing the underwear, the young rifleman shrugged. "I dunno, eight, I think."

"It's a gift, man!"

"And in here, it's Christmas! New bar tomorrow night, right?" the young rifleman yelled over the music.

"You got it, Cherry Boy!"

"Frequently," he said as he went out to join the women on the dance floor.

ENEMY, BY CHOICE

This is a story about prejudice and discrimination and about how people become our enemies. The Special Forces veteran who related this story did so because he wanted others to know about whom he fought and why. As an adviser to the montagnards, he was determined to help a people he found to be loyal, brave, and very much in need of what he had to offer.

What is moral is what you feel good after.
— ERNEST HEMINGWAY

It was an hour drive from the camp to the coast when there was a road to follow. Near the air base, they were given directions at the NCO club by two air force NCOs that were vague at best and something like a rehearsed routine anyway: "Follow the highway . . ."

"Fucked-up road is what it is," the second air force NCO said, while the first nodded in agreement.

"Yeah," he said, "follow the fucked-up road out to the river . . ."

"Sewer's more like it."

"Stinks to high heaven! Anyway, when you get there take the bridge . . ."

"Uh-uh," said the second. "The bridge is out, I think."

"Oh yeah. Right!" said the first airman. "Catch one of the navy's barges. I think they have barges running. Don't they?"

The second NCO nodded in agreement. "Yeah, barges," he said, echoing the first airman's remarks.

"Anyway, once you get on the other side of the river, get on the poor excuse for a road . . ."

"If it's open!"

"And drive up as best you can. I mean, if it ain't mined."

"Yeah. Sometimes there's land mines."

"Thanks," the Special Forces sergeant said, with more than a little uncertainty.

As road trips went, it was nothing special, but it was their first time to the big city, a supply run of sorts—a scrounging trip really—where they had managed to get a case of scotch for two AK-47s from an embassy employee and, from one of the guards, a swivel fan for an NVA belt buckle.

With business conducted and time to kill, the Special Forces sergeant decided there was time to do a little sightseeing in the former colonial French town. It was only a nine-mile drive through the historic city, so maybe a little sightseeing was in order after all. He figured it wouldn't hurt the montagnard mercenary driver, either, to see a little more than the small thatch-roofed highland village where he had been born, raised, and seldom left.

The American Green Beret knew it wouldn't hurt to combine a little R & R with the trip. The city was definitely an eye-opener, even to the American. Who knows? Maybe they'd find a mamma-san bar, at least a massage parlor, and the sergeant would get his ashes hauled and pay to get the yard laid, too. What the hookers charged was only a fraction of his Special Forces pay, but for the montagnard, it was damn near his everything! Besides, he was family. Well, sort of. A ceremonial blood brother, anyway, and the copper bracelet on his wrist said as much to anyone familiar with the montagnards.

After five months in country working with the montagnards, the American army Green Beret had come to appreciate and admire the tribal people, whom most Vietnamese looked upon with disdain. They reminded him of our Indians. After thirty days in the strike force village, the impression hadn't left him. From his training at Fort Bragg, he knew the montagnards were actually Malayo-Polynesian in origin and had lived in the area of South Vietnam long before the Vietnamese invaded the region and pushed them into the jungles and mountains. In fact, when the French found them and realized their potential, they called the montagnards "the Mountain People," even though not all of the thirty or so tribes who called themselves *dega*, "Sons of the Mountains," lived in the highlands.

After two hundred years of Vietnamese domination and on-again, off-again battles, they had reached a precarious peace and still managed to hold on to their tribal culture. They were the Rhade, Sudang, Jarai, or Mnong, or any of the subtribes and offshoots who traced their origins back to the larger tribes. They refused to give up their way of life and paid a price in the process as, slowly, they were edged out of their homelands—sometimes simply killed—by the invaders. They weren't represented in government, they were denied access to education and medical treatment, and they had their property and lands confiscated by both sides in the long war.

Befriended and respected by the Special Forces who, like the French, were quick to recognize the jungle fighting prowess behind the often gentle demeanor, the Montagnards were recruited to their cause at once.

The difficulty came in getting the montagnards to serve the Vietnamese, who not only discriminated against them in a way even the most redneck soldier would shake his head at but who, over the millennia, had systematically tried to destroy them. Old hatreds ran generations deep. It didn't help matters either for the Vietnamese to call them *moi*, a word that means savage and implies "animal," which was pretty much the way many Vietnamese viewed the montagnards. Less than human. Barbaric, too, or so many of the Vietnamese Special Forces officers had said.

The montagnards were also fierce, independent, and loyal to their tribes. But they weren't animals, just conquered peoples who preferred their own traditional lifestyle; a lifestyle alien to the Chinese-based Vietnamese and most Westerners as well. Like the birthing ritual in which the woman was required to venture alone into the jungle to have the baby. Ten days later, if everything was okay, she could return to have the father or grandfather name the baby and sacrifice a chicken or other animal to the gods. If the woman died at childbirth, then the baby, alive or dead, was buried with the woman's body in a hollowed log, again to appease the gods who could be vengeful if crossed.

They carved their farmlands from the dense rain forests and drank fermented rice wine and animals' blood in celebration of a good harvest or on such occasions as when they welcomed the Green Berets into their villages and lives. When the Green Berets first started working with the montagnards in the early sixties, the twentieth-century soldier came face-to-face with the barefoot, loincloth-wearing, stump-high warriors whose women dressed only in long black skirts and went around topless. The men hunted with bows and crossbows. They were expert woodsmen and hunters, and more important, they had a very long legacy of survival.

The American advisers liked what they found, and convinced the montagnards to work, in a roundabout way, for the Saigon government. Years later, after the montagnards had been serving the South Vietnamese government in the prolonged war, the South Vietnamese still made no secret of how they felt about them; they were still animals, still *moi*.

Resentment seemed to flow both ways when discrimination turned confrontational or bloody. Any romancing or fence-mending was done by the Americans, who hired and trained the yards as mercenaries. As reconnaissance or support forces, the montagnards were paid by the foreign advisers rather than by their Vietnamese government. Their twenty-dollar- to fifty-dollar-a-month salaries came from the U.S. government, specifically the Green Berets, who made no bones about admiring and respecting the wiry little bastards for their fighting abilities and staunch loyalty. The montagnards fought well, and they fought hard. Like them or not, the Vietnamese on both sides had to admit that. They were tough, and they were loyal to their tribe, their advisers. And their newfound knowledge of modern weapons and tactics made them dangerous, too. A fact the government in Saigon was well aware of. Periodically, the South Vietnamese would send out officers to command the montagnards. Often, the montagnards sent them packing or simply ran them out of the villages, threatening to kill them.

But war held priority over old arguments. There would be a time when the Saigon government would deal with the montagnards. After the Americans had left, perhaps. For the present, they were serving as allies.

Adopted in ceremonies into the tribes they advised, many of the Special Forces advisers, like the American sergeant, wore the thin metal bracelets that signified deep ties with the montagnards. This particular Green Beret sergeant was adopted into a particular family, and the blood ties bound him to montagnard obligations. He would never harm another montagnard, and he was sworn to protect his family from any enemy.

What the sergeant suspected, but couldn't prove, was that, while certain members of the tribe worked for the Viet Cong, they, too, were sworn to protect their American brothers. Any harm they directed was meant for the South Vietnamese or other Americans.

Most, though, served the Green Berets exclusively. Like the little yard who was the sergeant's twenty-year-old man Friday, his jungle Tonto sidekick and little blood brother, who had saved his life at least once, twice maybe, and who became the sergeant's jeep driver after one or two clutches. What the fuck! Driving the jeep gave the yard status, and once the silly but likable moon-faced son of a bitch got the hang of speed shifting, the clutch didn't really matter too much anyhow.

As combat soldiers, they weren't really all that concerned with the rumors that the Viet Cong might be operating in the region between the camp and the city because, hell, they had always operated in the area! Any area! At times, especially during incoming rocket attacks, when the strategic targets were hit with more than usual frequency, it became evident that many of the South Vietnamese who worked in the American compounds cleaning hootches or doing laundry also worked for the Viet Cong at one time or another or supplied information the Cong needed. So if the road wasn't safe, then it probably wasn't safe for unarmed soldiers rather than an all-out ambush. It wasn't unusual for the Viet Cong to set up a makeshift roadside tax collection site or recruiting station where they took what and who they wanted.

However, it wasn't all that prudent to open up on armed Americans, let alone a Green Beret soldier with a *moi*. At least not during the peak travel hours when everybody and their brother used the highways. The Viet Cong weren't generally suicidal, and they well understood planning and timing in warfare.

The key to traveling in country by roadway, the Special Forces sergeant knew, was to travel in daylight hours, preferably after 10 A.M. and before last light, which in the brief twilight period before sunset added a whole new meaning to the term rush hour.

That day the primary concern was traffic. The road was busy with the usual smoke-belching buses, a variety of allied military vehicles, trucks, three-wheel vans, and the throng of motor scooters and bicycles, all going to and from the coastal city. And, like most traffic in Vietnam, the rules of the road were either individually waived, made up, or not very well-enforced or understood.

On the outskirts of the city, the traffic got heavier, and the going became ridiculously slow. Too many stop-and-goes for the sergeant's liking. The yard wasn't thrilled either, so with the sergeant's approval, he made a detour to get out of the mess. Wheeling around a less confused corner, the two left the sound of blaring horns and yelling drivers in the distance only to find an equally congested road less than two miles ahead. Everyone seemed to be on the roads and highways, and they'd long since given up on finding the shortcut to town. Just getting out of the traffic had become the real challenge. Vendors and stalls spilled over onto the already crowded street, and the wheeled traffic jockeyed around them.

"Fuck!" the yard said, correctly using one of the few English words he had learned from the American sergeant.

The simple nine-mile drive became an ordeal, and any thought of what he intended to do once they arrived at their destination was replaced by anger at the frustration of the journey. It was hard to think about getting laid when your day so far had been fucked. The traffic was a mess, and the yard shot for any openings he could find.

When an oncoming pedicab swerved in front of them to scoot around a three-wheeled motorbike, the yard yanked the jeep's wheel hard to the left just as an old man leading a sixty-pound pig on a rope stepped out from an alley.

"Shit! Look out!" the sergeant yelled. Too late; the jeep's bumper barely missed the old man but caught the pig square on the ham hip, tossing and twisting him under the wheel with a resounding *thump-whump*, quickly followed by a terrified squeal.

"Fuck! Fuck!" the yard said, jumping on the brakes, switching the jeep to *off*, and leaping out of the driver's seat to see about the old man's pig. The dying animal lay moaning beneath the wheel well. Its hips were crushed, and blood was spilling from its anus.

"Fuck!" the yard said again, looking at the sergeant for support and then back at the broken body of the large pig. The old man was moaning along with the almost dead animal. The old man's brown eyes were glazed and watering in pain. This was a bad omen, and bad things would happen to him now.

"Get the aid kit!" the sergeant yelled to the yard, who hurriedly scrambled back into the jeep to retrieve the small olive drab emergency kit beneath the passenger's seat. The Special Forces sergeant wasn't certain what good, if any, it would do, but appearances sometimes counted for something in the eyes of those who viewed you as outsiders. The deed might be done, but how one reacted or responded to the damage often mitigated the animosity. Or so he hoped.

By the time he retrieved the kit, the Special Forces NCO had managed to pull the old man's pig from beneath the jeep and in front of the vehicle, the reasoning being that the parked jeep would provide a sheltered cove around which traffic would flow. But logic in Vietnam didn't always work well. The traffic simply adjusted to the new problem and, at times, moved precariously close before veering away, after gawking at the dying animal. Many had seen worse.

A small crowd, made up mostly of bicycle traffic and nearby vendors, began to assemble, and someone yelled something in Vietnamese about an animal killing an animal, while somebody else laughed. But it was the piercing scream of an old woman that was heard above the din. A small, stooped woman, perhaps the old man's wife, pushed through the bystanders, wailing as she squatted to inspect the damage. The wealth of the two old Asians lay bleeding in the busy street.

"I'm sorry," the yard said to the old woman, who looked at him with malice. Her wailing turned to a steady sob. The old man was still in shock, and the significance of the loss hadn't set in. But the woman knew.

There was nothing anyone could do to save the pig, and salvaging what was left would be the next hurdle to get over. Slaughtering any animal required care and something more than a littered street, and the old woman sobbed about that, too. Not only had their pig been killed, but it would be wasted!

When the Vietnamese police jeep arrived, the two police officers, the "White Mice" as they were known to Americans because of their white shirts, white gloves, pistol belts, and shoulder boards, sauntered out of the vehicle to survey the scene. The senior policeman in charge quickly reached the same conclusion as the old woman. He drew his .45-caliber pistol and shot the dying animal once in the head. The pig's body bucked from the bullet, then, after a few tremors, lay still. The single shot was enough to disperse most of the small crowd. To some, carnage on any level was always show.

"You pay for pig!" the senior policeman in charge said to the Special Forces sergeant after he had heard what had happened from the old man and a witness. In the heavy heat of the early afternoon, the open court was in session. The case was closed. All that remained now were the plea bargains.

Although the yard had been driving, the police officer wasn't about to talk to him. Nor did it matter that it was an accident and they were forced to swerve when they did. The pedicab was long gone. Besides, Americans had money. The American sergeant would pay.

Having heard about similar situations and not wanting things to get out of hand, the Special Forces sergeant decided that paying for the dead animal was the prudent thing to do. Now it was just a matter of negotiation.

"How much?" he said, knowing the dickering was about to start. "For the small pig, I mean?" He had a little over one hundred dollars MPC on him as well as forty dollars American and maybe another twenty dollars in Vietnamese dong. When you killed someone's animal in Vietnam, you not only paid for the actual market cost of the animal but for the possible generations of progeny the dead animal was likely to produce.

"Two hundred dollars MPC!" the senior police officer said immediately. That was awfully high, but he was just setting the upper limits for the bargaining process.

The American sergeant shook his head. "I don't have

that much. It's a small pig, and maybe worth fifty dollars MPC?" he said, which only angered the police officer. But the rage was feigned and unconvincing, and after offers and counteroffers, a deal was finally struck.

Eighty dollars in MPC or military payment certificates and twenty dollars in Vietnamese dong would do it. They were gone. He knew that much. That would take care of the dead pig and maybe satisfy the old couple. Still, he knew it wasn't over. There was the matter of inconveniencing the police, which would eat up the first twenty dollars American. That would leave the American twenty dollars MPC and twenty dollars American. Maybe. The first deal was reached, but there was always something more.

Surprisingly, the senior police officer reluctantly accepted the offer. The money was transferred to the senior police officer, who didn't seem to be in a hurry to hand it over to the old couple. "You go now!" the junior officer said, dismissing them with a smirk as the senior officer counted the money. "Go!"

Knowing his part in the street play, the montagnard remained dutifully quiet as he began to load the dead pig into the jeep.

"What are you doing?" demanded the senior police officer in Vietnamese, but in a tone that even the American could recognize as indignation.

"Loading our pig," the montagnard replied calmly. "We have paid for him. He is ours. We will eat the meat."

The police officer shook his head and smiled. "It is not yours, leave it, *moi.*" The Special Forces adviser had watched the exchange with more than a little concern because it was easy to see where the argument would go. When he heard the policeman call the montagnard an animal, he stepped in to cool the situation.

The facial muscles in the montagnard's small, round face were taut while the policeman's neck cord was jumping from the angry blood rushing through his head. Obviously, the *moi* didn't know his place. "Why do you steal our pig?" he asked in a calm voice that was slowly turning angry.

"Let's stay cool. Everything's fine," the American adviser said, with hands opened and waving. Only the senior policeman wasn't having any of it. The yard's insolence was obvious, and the *moi* didn't know his place. The junior policeman had his pistol drawn and used it to wave the American back.

The sergeant wasn't a key player anymore. "Stay cool, man. Cool," he said, as the younger policeman backed him away from the jeep and the M-16 rifles between the two front seats.

The senior policeman was yelling again, using a torrent of insults that the yard probably didn't fully understand but whose meaning was apparent, even to the American. They were in deep shit now. Both of them.

When the yard returned an insult, the senior officer pulled out his pistol and began waving it dangerously at the defiant and still unrepentant montagnard.

"Don't give him a reason," the adviser said, hoping to God the mercenary understood their position, and then turning to the policemen, broke into a wide smile. "Hey look! We're sorry! Really sorry. It won't happen again, sir. Okay? It's a misunderstanding. That's all. I'm certain we can correct it by paying a fine. A *big* fine."

The ploy seemed to be working until the senior policeman suddenly backhanded the montagnard across the face with the heavy pistol. The skin on the left side of the yard's cheek was cut to the eye and immediately began to swell and discolor as the policeman leveled the barrel at the yard. Blood spilled from his small face and fell down his sun-bleached uniform that consisted of an old American army shirt, shorts, and tennis shoes.

The rifles were still in the front of the jeep, only there was no getting to them in time if push came to shove, and push was rocking their balance as it was.

"I'm an American, and he works for me!"

"Fuck you, G.I.!" the senior policeman replied. "You see! I shoot him if I want!" he yelled, turning his attention back to the montagnard while the second policeman was taking his cue from his superior. *"Moi!"* laughed the senior policeman, firing another round into the head of the already dead pig and laughing as he fired a second and third time. The head shattered and was unrecognizable. The policeman turned the pistol barrel to the montagnard's face and yelled at him again only to find the montagnard no longer resisting and very much in his place. "You see? You see!"

There was no mistaking the resignation and fear in the yard's deep-set eyes, but there was something more that maybe the police officer missed but the American adviser picked up on.

"I see!" said the American. "I see we're wrong! You're right. We're sorry. Very sorry. Please. I want to show you how sorry we are," he said, pointing to the jeep and the goods stored in the back. "There is some whiskey for you, for your trouble. Please take it as a gift, and we'll leave. Take it!" he said, again gesturing to the jeep while he could see the wheels spinning behind the senior policeman's eyes. This was his out, and he knew it. He could kill the *moi* but not the American. Not directly, anyway. There were other ways.

"It's just a misunderstanding, sir. That's all," the Special Forces sergeant said again, thinking *you fuck* but adding *sir* one more time.

With a sharp command, the senior policeman sent the

junior officer to inspect the jeep and, once done, had the man carry the whiskey to their own vehicle. The junior officer whispered something to the senior officer, who nodded gravely, and then had the younger man return to the American jeep. It didn't take long to see what he was doing. The *son of a bitch* was removing the magazines from the M-16s, pulling the charging handles back, and ejecting the remaining round in the chamber from both weapons. Then he took the extra magazines and the fragmentation grenades in the web gear, leaving the travelers defenseless, which was the senior officer's plan: it was getting late, and the two outsiders could take their chances with the Viet Cong.

"You go now! Go!" the senior police officer barked. With empty rifles, the ride back to the nearest American base would be uneasy at best.

The fucker is leaving us unarmed! the American thought and started to say something, thought better of it, and instead returned to the jeep, starting its engine.

"Let's go," he said wearily as the montagnard climbed into the passenger's seat beside him with blood still streaming down the side of his face. He didn't seem to notice the pain, just the insult.

"Here, let's take a look at that!" he said, letting the engine idle as he handed his blood brother the first-aid kit, and he dug around for something to put on it. They had settled on a quick-fix gauze patch and several strands of tape. However, the show wasn't over.

"No go! You clean the animal and put pig in jeep," the junior officer said, pointing to his own vehicle while the senior officer smiled over his shoulder, watching as he offered the old man and woman half the dong he had taken from the American. The Green Beret sergeant started to climb out, but the junior police officer shook his head and pointed at the montagnard with his pistol.

"Him!" he yelled, practicing a little of his own abuse of power. It was about saving and losing face and affirming one's role in the process. The clang of the Vietnamese bayonet the junior policeman threw toward the dead animal was maybe what it appeared to be or perhaps a death sentence.

The montagnard looked at the American for a moment and handed him back the first-aid kit before getting back out of the jeep. The small bandage they had in place would be enough to stop the bleeding and maybe take care of it for now, but the yard would need stitches.

"I can help with your pig," the American said. The senior officer laughed and waved him on. With the two of them that far from their own jeep, if they tried something with the knife then that would be reason enough to kill them both. The senior police officer laid his .45 pistol in his lap.

The montagnard knelt down and tried to find something in the dead animal's shattered head to grab ahold of. When he had a grip, he cut the pig's throat with a surprisingly easy cut and then sliced the animal up the underside from the anus to the chest cavity, spilling the viscera onto himself and the streets.

"Continue," the officer said in Vietnamese.

Reaching in with his hands, the montagnard pulled out the rest of the intestines and organs, his hands bloody and smelling foul in the hot sun. The American adviser was beside him, holding open the meat when the odor overpowered him, and he felt the bile coming up from his stomach. Barely turning away in time, he vomited over himself, and wiped at the bile that fell from his nose.

The Vietnamese policemen and the small crowd were laughing at his misfortune. A few were pointing. Heading back to the jeep, he retched again, feeling the stomach acid caught in his throat. Bracing himself between the jeep and the street, he breathed slowly until he was certain the spell was over. The montagnard removed his shirt and handed it to the American, who used it to wipe his face. He laid it on the passenger's seat as the yard came around to the jeep, reached into the first-aid kit, and found something for the American. He settled for a Compazine spanual, a muscle relaxant. Taking the canteen from his web gear, the montagnard handed it to the sergeant, who took the pill and a long drink from the canteen.

The yard placed the first-aid box back under the seat before he returned to the dead animal. The sergeant soon joined him. When they had finally finished, the two struggled under the weight of the carcass and carried it to the back of the police jeep, where they laid it down carefully under the scrutiny of the Vietnamese policemen. Pig shit, blood, and entrails covered the two, giving the policemen something new to smile about.

"Now you go!" the junior officer yelled as the senior policeman settled into his seat. The pistol was still very much in sight in his hand resting on his lap.

Climbing into their own jeep, the American started the engine and eased out into the thinning traffic. Much of the day was gone, and people were hurrying to be elsewhere. The night was coming, and so were the shadows. A cold chill sprang from the base of his neck and ran down his spine. The yard hadn't said anything about what else he had removed from the first-aid box or how he had inserted it in the carcass of the pig. Instead, he took his canteen and slowly poured the water over his hands, then handed the canteen to the American, who did the same. And the Vietnamese wondered why montagnards would go over to the Viet Cong, the American thought.

"Fuck 'em," the Green Beret said, finding a main street that showed the highway farther up the road. The yard had taken the grenade from beneath the seat and concealed it in the balled shirt and then slipped it into the pig's neck as they were cleaning it. He wedged it firmly in place, knowing the spoon on the grenade wouldn't slip for a while. Maybe a pothole or two or maybe when they took a corner a little too fast, and then the grenade would explode. With the pin removed, the spoon would dislodge, and the two Vietnamese police would only be seconds from dying.

The NCO had come to Vietnam hoping he was going to make a difference. Nothing big, but something that might help. This was one of the few times when he actually believed it and hated an enemy he hadn't expected to find.

"Fuck 'em!" he said to himself.

When the grenade exploded, the policemen would be wounded or killed and more than likely their deaths would be attributed to enemy attack. The report would be correct. In a way.

When the Green Beret sergeant found the main highway, he stepped on the gas and shifted into a higher gear, leaving the kill zone and the real war behind him in a swirl of dust.

NOTHING!

Official accounts often left a great deal to the imagination, but for the soldier fighting the war, the truth had a way of making itself known. At times it did so with such intensity and impact that the lie was too big to cover up.

The only thing new in this world is the history you don't know.
—HARRY S. TRUMAN

"The TOC's on the line, Ell-Tee," the radioman said to the platoon leader. The TOC was the tactical operations center back at the base camp.

"Hold up!" the lieutenant ordered, holding his right arm up and bringing the three squads behind him to a halt, while the word was passed along for the point squad to stop in place.

The reconnaissance platoon was twenty-two soldiers in strength and strung out along a high-speed trail in the disputed border region that separated Vietnam from Cambodia. The dispute was a moot point, since the Viet Cong had the strength and firepower to keep the Cambodian army from forcing the issue.

The recon platoon's job was to find the Viet Cong strongholds in the area, pick a fight, and then hold out for infantry support as the helicopter gunships from the 1st of the 9th Cav rolled in on the enemy soldiers.

"It's Six Actual," the radioman said, handing the radio's handset back to the lieutenant.

Six Actual was the unit's commander, who explained the situation as the lieutenant listened gravely.

"Roger," he said when Six Actual had finished. "Break," the lieutenant added hurriedly. "Alpha, Bravo, and Delta. You copy? Over." The lieutenant was asking if each of the three squad leaders in the platoon had monitored the last radio transmission.

"Roger," came the replies, one after another.

"Then get your people down and behind cover. Do it now!" the lieutenant ordered as he sneaked a quick glance skyward but saw nothing through the triple canopy but occasional patches of pale blue sky.

"What is it?" a new guy in the point squad asked while a war-weary, twenty-year-old specialist four ignored the question, scooting in closer to the base of a tree and drawing his knees up to his chest in the combat fetal position.

"Keep your head down!" he said while doing just that.

"Why?" asked the new guy. But the answer soon came whistling through the trees and surrounding vegetation as a rumbling grew louder, and the ground began to buck and jump. White-hot shrapnel flew like boomerangs, slicing tree limbs, branches, and leaves. Hundreds of 750-pound bombs pulverized the target site while the concussion and shrapnel carried over into the buffer zone. The reconnaissance platoon was safe, but just barely.

The rumbling seemed to go on forever, and then, as though on cue, it stopped. The jungle was awkwardly quiet; even the wildlife was too stunned to respond.

The squawking of the radio and busy commo traffic could be heard through the underbrush as Six Actual and the lieutenant were calling for situation reports. Someone in the 3d Squad had received a burn when hot shrapnel landed on his exposed hand. It was a minor wound.

"The air force almost killed us!" the new guy said as the specialist four listened to the squad's radioman, who was sitting a few feet to his left and looking frustrated as he slowly shook his head.

"Naw, it was nothing," said the radioman, the sarcasm lingering like the dust cloud that was settling over the countryside.

The new guy looked to the specialist four for support, while the specialist four waited for the radioman to finish, but the new guy wouldn't let him.

"That was a B-52 strike, wasn't it?" he said while the radioman shook his head.

"No, it wasn't. Because that's Cambodia," said the radioman, pointing in the direction of the target site.

"So?"

The radioman laughed at the new guy's response. "So we don't drop bombs on Cambodia."

"It sure as shit sounded and felt like a bomb run!"

"It was nothing."

"But we almost got killed!"

"No shit!" said the specialist four. "But it was still nothing. Officially, we're not bombing Cambodia because the Viet Cong say they're not in Cambodia. Never mind they're lying about being there and we're lying about bombing the hell out of them."

"That's nuts!"

"There it is."

The new guy still didn't understand, but then the specialist four wasn't certain he did either. "It doesn't make sense!" the new guy said.

"No shit. Welcome to the real war!"

From March 1969 to May 1970, the United States Air Force secretly conducted Operation Menu, dropping 108,837 tons of bombs on Cambodia's border regions. On July 30, 1974, the House Judiciary Committee voted to impeach President Richard Nixon for not informing Congress of the top-secret bombings, and although the measure failed, the move added to the pressure that eventually caused Nixon to resign from his office.

READY, SET . . .

C-4 is a thick, white, plastic, doughlike explosive most commonly used in claymore antipersonnel mines and as a general-purpose-demolitions explosive. A stable explosive, it could easily be carried without fear of its going off without a blasting cap or, as rumor had it, unless a G.I. used it to light a fire, for C rations, say, and he tried to put it out by stomping on it.

The Training NCO at Fort Benning, Georgia, was adamant about the proper use of C-4. "It's a fine explosive so long as you take the necessary precautions," he explained to the class of soldiers during the hands-on portion of the block of instruction concerning explosives.

"It won't accidentally go off; you need a blasting cap or detonation device to detonate it. You can drop it, kick it, throw it down, and nothing will happen. The nice thing, too, is that you can mold it into any shape you like and cut trees in half, or hide it on the side of a trail and wait until Charlie comes along and then detonate it and blow him into confetti!" he said before taking the soldiers out on the range and showing them how to use it in a variety of ways.

All across the nation, infantry and engineer soldiers were receiving similar instruction in places like Fort Dix,

New Jersey; Fort Jackson, South Carolina; Fort Lewis, Washington; Fort Ord, California; Fort Bragg, North Carolina; and the home of the infantry, Fort Benning, Georgia.

The G.I.'s in attendance were told not to use C-4 to heat their C rations or coffee in the field. "We know people are using it for that, breaking off pieces from blocks, even removing it from claymore antipersonnel mines, because it burns well," said the instructors.

"The trouble is, it's possible that when you try to put it out by stomping on it, it'll blow your toes, boot, and leg halfway to Saigon! Don't *do* it, people!"

G.I.'s nodded and said they wouldn't. But when they got to Vietnam, that's exactly what some did. Staff Sergeant Grover "Gene" Sprague had even seen a new guy light up an entire block of C-4, turning the dark evening jungle into a well-lighted backdrop.

"It looked like sunrise," he said, "and we all scrambled to quickly bury it. If the Viet Cong didn't know we were there before that happened, they sure did afterward." Of course, the soldiers didn't stomp on the burning block of C-4 because of the warning they had received back in the World.

However, there were others who decided to put the theory to the test in ways even the Fort Benning instructors hadn't imagined.

"Ready?" one of the G.I.'s yelled at the soldier climbing on top of the platoon hootch.

"No," said the soldier as he crab-crawled into position to keep from sliding off the corrugated tin roof. Below, standing in a semicircle, the G.I.'s were waiting for the man to get into position. The block of C-4 had already been ignited and was engulfed in flames.

"Both feet, right?" called the man on the roof as he glanced down at the burning explosive.

"Yeah," replied a spectator from the ground. "Ready? Set? *Go!*"

A chant rose from those below as the soldier pushed off and landed squarely on the burning C-4. The pressure didn't put out the fire, nor did it detonate the C-4. The G.I.'s laughed and handed the man a beer.

"Airborne!" someone yelled. Of course, if it had gone off, then all of those in the semicircle would certainly have been airborne.

Heat and enough pressure would set any explosive off, and often with less than, say, a leap of faith.

A GOOD AMBUSH

On January 27, 1962, Robert McNamara, the secretary of defense, forwarded a memorandum from the Joint Chiefs of Staff to President John F. Kennedy urging him to deploy American forces in South Vietnam. Citing the domino theory, the leading military generals and admirals vehemently argued that failure to deploy American forces would only delay what eventually would have to be done and make the job all the more difficult. So, when Richard Keeton went off to Vietnam shortly after Kennedy gave the go-ahead, he served as an enlisted adviser to the South Vietnamese Army, with the blessing of Camelot and a boon that would later prove to be just as mythical as those of King Arthur. Keeton did two tours of duty in the war and today is active in veterans affairs and community services.

> The greatest lesson in life is to know that even
> fools are right sometimes.
> —WINSTON CHURCHILL

In the spring of 1963, most of the world, with the exception of France, couldn't tell you where Indochina was, let alone find the tiny nation of Vietnam on a map. The French had lost their bitter colonial war nine years earlier, and the United States was in the process of taking a more active role in the region. For years, the United States had covertly helped bankroll the French in their struggle and, in 1963, were squarely behind the Diem regime in Saigon, which opposed the reunification efforts of Ho Chi Minh.

For the United States, that wasn't a difficult wedge to drive. There was no love lost between the North and the South, and traditional anger and resentments were hundreds of years old, so when the South Vietnamese government requested more than financial assistance from the United States, President John F. Kennedy responded by sending military assistance advisory groups, or MAAG teams, from the army's newly established Special Forces, the Green Berets.

Cpl. Richard Keeton was the enlisted half of a two-man advisory team, and when he arrived in country, a briefing NCO—a stocky, leather-faced veteran of two previous wars—offered a few words of advice.

"First of all," he said to the young corporal, "don't think you're going to pump these people up with God-and-country speeches, except for maybe the Cao Dai, who worship damn near everybody!

"The others, and there are plenty of other clusters of people here, got a variety of gods, and we don't look like none of them. Besides, they've been fighting each other for a thousand years or so, give or take a century. Some of the soldiers you'll be *advising*," he added, in a tone heavy with sarcasm and bordering on anger, "are corrupt, lazy, worthless pieces of water-buffalo shit, who tolerate you only because you represent Santa Claus to them.

"You can buy and sell rank in this army for the price of a smoked ham, and the sad part is that some of the soldiers who are under the Saigon Army command are some of the most gung ho and well meaning you'll ever find. *Some*," he said, emphasizing the point.

"The rest, well, besides the ones who don't trust either their own officers or the enemy because they've been fucked over by both sides for damn near ever, like I said, they only listen to us because of the goodies we have to offer, such as vehicles, weapons, and equipment and shit. Not to mention the televisions, cameras, and jewelry found in our soon-to-be-built post exchanges.

"When you're out on patrol, that is, *if* you can get your South Vietnamese Army hosts to go on patrol in the first place, then watch out for the enemy. Keep an eye on your back, too, because some of the soldiers in these units you'll be advising are the enemy or have relatives in the Viet Cong.

"Let's see. Have I forgotten anything? Oh yeah, don't expect too much sympathy from the local populace, either, because foreigners have been screwing them over for years, too. We're just the latest folks to arrive. Any questions?"

Keeton shook his head, adding, "Other than that, Mrs. Lincoln, how did you like the play?"

"You got it, Corporal."

The informal welcoming speech, followed by a more formal briefing covering the specifics of the mission and their roles in it, was straightforward. They were advisers. "You advise," said the briefing NCO. "You try to work with them on strategy and tactics or, say, which part of a grenade to throw. Hopefully, too, you can get the South Vietnamese Army unit out in the bush and away from their rear-area camps and teach them to take the fighting seriously. No problem for you young studs."

However, there was a problem, and the difficulty came when the young officer, who was the second American attached to the MAAG team, and Corporal Keeton realized the personnel of the Vietnamese Army company they were assigned to weren't exactly thrilled about finding the enemy or winning the conflict anytime soon.

The South Vietnamese captain in charge of the infantry company seemed to be indifferent to the Americans' advice, which through his interpreter—a thin-faced, wiry little man who reminded Keeton of a ferret—the captain frequently chose to ignore. Physical fitness training was out of the question, as were map reading, jungle training, reconnaissance missions, road marches, small-arms familiarization, and of course patrolling, unless the captain wanted to ransack a nearby village or two for booty. Ambushes were also out, which didn't leave the advisers much else to offer.

"Captain say, too dangerous," explained the ferret interpreter. "Too dangerous, he say! Much too dangerous. Too, too dangerous."

Frustrated and more than a little annoyed after too many ignored suggestions and disregarded advice, the two Americans decided to try another tack: blackmail. Sort of.

The unit was due for a resupply of American goods and equipment, which meant the Vietnamese captain would soon have new merchandise for the black market, a fact not lost on either of the advisers, who couldn't help but notice that when the supplies were dropped off, one third had mysteriously disappeared by a day or two later, and that a day or two after that, the captain disappeared for the weekend, and the ferret seemed to bet a little more when he gambled.

The key lay in the resupply mission, and the advisers knew it.

"So here's what we do," explained the lieutenant to the corporal. "We delay the resupply, telling the little fucker that if we don't go out on at least one combat operation, then we won't be supplied. We'll say that our people—no, better yet, our *general* in Saigon is unhappy with our efforts and that we have to offer him something, a patrol at least."

"You think it'll work?" asked Keeton.

"It's worth a shot, which damn well may be the only one we'll see on this tour!"

When the American officer explained the situation to the Vietnamese captain through the ferret, Corporal Keeton nodded in solemn agreement. "He's unhappy!" added Keeton. "Beaucoup unhappy. No mission, no supplies."

Reluctantly, and with much discussion between the captain and the ferret, the two agreed on one combat operation.

"One mission," said the ferret.

"A night ambush!" said the American officer.

"Day!" rejoined the interpreter.

"One platoon."

"No, the entire company," said the ferret without consulting the captain.

"Let me guess, too dangerous?" asked the lieutenant.

The ferret nodded. "Camp not safe with one platoon gone. Too dangerous. Many VC."

"Okay, but we pick the ambush site," added the American.

"You pick, but the captain in charge. He say too dangerous for people who do not know Vietnam." Keeton wanted to tell the little shit that maybe they would get to know it a lot better if they went out on patrol once in a while, but he let it ride. Things were as good as they were going to get.

"No problem. The captain's still in charge on tomorrow's ambush. Say, first light?"

"No, too dangerous," said the ferret. "Must plan. Next week, sometime. After supplies come."

The lieutenant held firm. "*Before* supplies come. No patrol, no supplies. How about the day after tomorrow?"

The ferret sulked, and they had their answer.

In a makeshift briefing in the captain's bunker, the Americans offered the proposed ambush site, a fork in a jungle trail a few klicks north at a natural ford in a small river. "It's a good spot. It's a main trail that comes out in the open to cross the stream. And maybe, just maybe, we can hide the entire company on this side, not to mention his worship here."

While the Vietnamese interpreter's English was passable, his sense of sarcasm had not fully developed, at least not in two languages. "His worship," the ferret reasoned, sounding respectful. "Captain say okay, but just one patrol because . . ."

"Too dangerous?" asked the lieutenant.

"Correct."

"Now how did I know that?" asked the officer, looking to Keeton, who only shrugged.

So on the day of the ambush, as the warm morning gave way to a searing afternoon, Keeton and the lieutenant led the Vietnamese company toward the proposed ambush site. It would take an hour of walking and, knowing the captain wasn't about to stay in the jungle overnight, any ambush would only have an hour or so window of opportunity. After that, the captain would order their return to camp.

"Well, at least it's an ambush, sir," Keeton said. "And it's a good spot."

The officer shrugged. The corporal was right, though. It was a good ambush site. One of the few real plausible locations, because the Viet Cong were active in the area, and it was one of the few natural crossing sites.

The several days' opportunity, and the advantage of being in place in the early morning, were lost. They knew that was because the captain wanted to make certain the Viet Cong had left the area. After all, they tended to move in the early morning and just prior to sunset.

By the time Keeton and the lieutenant got to the stream, they were far ahead of the others, and they hadn't moved all that fast. The jungle that wrapped around them was surprisingly dense, so the two Americans checked out the immediate area and then crossed the stream to see what natural cover they had to work with. The underbrush was carpet-thick with vines and limbs interwoven like a green-and-brown wall hanging, but the trail showed signs of recent enemy use, hours-old footprints, and bicycle tracks. It was a good spot, so they waited. And waited. And waited.

"Anytime now would be nice," Keeton said to the young officer, the frustration evident on his face. Staring at the stream while tossing twigs in the slow-flowing water, the lieutenant nodded. He had intended to save the world from communism, beginning with Southeast Asia, but lately wondered if maybe it took more patience.

"Think they'll show?"

"If they do, then it'll only be because they want us to lead them back to camp," the officer replied. A sudden *crack* caught their attention, and the two Green Berets whirled around, weapons ready, studying the jungle wall. Tense seconds later, a gecko lizard croaked in the distance, and they let down their guard.

As the day wore on, the heat rose. Finding shade, the

two advisers settled in, still waiting for the others to show. Forty minutes or so later, Vietnamese voices could be heard moving down the trail.

"Can't be Viet Cong," Keeton said. "They wouldn't make that much noise—"

"—or be stupid enough to move this late in the day."

As the first South Vietnamese soldier cleared the bend, he spied the two Americans and then grinned and waved. The soldier behind him was talking to the soldier behind him, oblivious to the threat of combat.

The second Vietnamese soldier carried his rifle in what could only be described as "the luggage grip," and scratched his ass when he saw the two Americans on the other side of the river.

Like a Keystone Cops parody, the soldiers walking behind the first two soldiers bumped into each other and then bunched up on the bank of the slow-flowing stream, coming to a halt and refusing to go any farther.

After some discussion, the luggage-grip soldier used his rifle to test the depth of the crossing site only to fall in the water. He was spitting and sputtering as he emerged. Laughter erupted from the onlookers on the bank of the river while Keeton and the lieutenant just shook their heads in frustration.

"Come on!" the lieutenant called to the soldiers as annoyed frowns spread across their faces at the thought of having to wade across the stream. The unfortunate soldier tried to climb the stream bank but tumbled back and disappeared momentarily beneath the surface.

The second volley of laughter that erupted was cut short as the first Viet Cong machine-gun rounds tore across the trees above the Vietnamese soldiers.

The gunfire seemed to be coming from behind Keeton and the officer. The sudden surprise of enemy small-arms fire sent the South Vietnamese soldiers scrambling for cover as they returned fire in myriad directions.

Within minutes, Keeton knew the Viet Cong had quickly and quietly slipped back into the rain forest, but the South Vietnamese soldiers continued to fire at random, hitting everything but their intended targets. The trick was keeping down and surviving their small-arms fire. Finally, Keeton and the young officer yelled at them to cease fire. "VC gone! VC gone!" Keeton shouted until the soldiers got the message, and the small-arms fire across the bank subsided.

"VC gone?" the ferret yelled as heads peeked out to make sure they had indeed left the area. The South Vietnamese point man stood up and waved again but refused to go near the stream bank again.

"Come on!" the young officer yelled, motioning the South Vietnamese soldiers forward to pursue the fleeing Viet Cong.

"No," replied the South Vietnamese interpreter from somewhere back across the stream, a frightened voice wafting through the foliage. "Too dangerous. Captain say, you come back."

"Unbelievable," Keeton said, shaking his head and looking around the ambush site. "Think we'll ever get them back out on patrol again?"

"With a crowbar maybe. Still, at least the Viet Cong thought it was a good ambush site."

"Yes, sir, and they did a pretty damn good job sneaking up on us, too. Real professional. Now, if only they'd stayed a little longer . . ."

"Uh-huh, and spread out in an L-shape . . ."

". . . and concentrated their fire . . ."

"That's right, Corporal. Then they would have had one hell of an ambush."

"You think maybe the French forgot to tell us something?"

"You mean, like which side actually gives a shit about winning?"

"Yes, sir. Little things like that."

"*Oui*," said the lieutenant. "Come on. Let's go before the Viet Cong figure out they screwed up less than our guys did."

THE TALISMAN

While most people will say they don't really believe in luck, they'll still buy lottery tickets, take weekend trips to Reno, Las Vegas, or Atlantic City, or even wish on an occasional star. While chance or coincidence can account for most seemingly lucky events, there is still that small percentage that defies all logic or reason. In the following story, luck comes in the form of a flip-top lighter.

Coincidence is luck without believing.
—ANONYMOUS

They were called Thunder Runs, high-speed gauntlet races by the mechanized infantry units of the army's 1st Infantry Division along Highway 13, northwest of Saigon. The tactic was used to throw off the Viet Cong and North Vietnamese Army units, which had frequently staged ambushes along the remote highway and the secondary roads that fed into it.

The name Thunder Run came from the Big Red One's fire support bases—named Thunder One, Thunder Two, and Thunder Three—that dotted the route from Quan Loi south to Lai Khe.

The fire support bases were outposts that doubled as

speed bumps for the highway that served as one of the main off ramps of the infamous Ho Chi Minh trail.

The North Vietnamese Army units and Viet Cong who operated openly in force in the border-province area were well aware that the Americans were usually cautious when they moved en masse, and since their tanks and tracked vehicles could only use the serviceable roads, the enemy commanders planned their attacks and ambushes accordingly. What they didn't plan on were the Americans' abruptly changing tactics, replacing the slow, cautious approach for an up-the-middle run, with the tanks leading the way, using recon by fire to recon suspicious-looking areas as they roared on. The grunts called it driving on rock and roll.

The Thunder Runs had accounted for more than a few broken enemy ambushes and had prevented the NVA and Viet Cong from waging a successful ambush campaign. Cautious, the enemy needed time to analyze and react to the new tactic. But if this tactic was hard on the enemy, then it was equally hard on the nerves of the mechanized infantrymen; at any time, a recon by fire could erupt into a deadly battle.

Midway through his tour of duty, Sp4. Darrel Pilat still hadn't gotten used to it. Even as his unit aligned its vehicles to begin another run, Pilat's palms got damp, and the adrenaline surge formed a balloon in his chest that wouldn't subside for hours. He had been in his share of firefights, and so far, he had been lucky.

Subconsciously, he rubbed his thumb over his flip-top lighter for luck and then laughed when he realized what he was doing. It was a silly gesture, and although his rational mind told him there was no such thing as luck, let alone a good-luck charm, something deeper and more primordial told him that luck did indeed exist. However, Vietnam had also taught him that luck was fickle. What else could explain why one soldier lived while another next in line, even beside him, died? Combat was often a matter of inches to live or seconds to die, with an unseen hand holding the yardstick and watch.

Pilat made the mistake once of letting others know the lighter was his good-luck charm. Several of the new arrivals laughed at the notion, while a few of the veterans nodded in quiet understanding. Even a veteran NCO said, "Whatever works. I mean, for a cheap-ass piece of crap lighter. You should get yourself a Zippo. If you want a good-luck charm that'll last, a Zippo will last."

Pilat held on to the inexpensive lighter anyway for a few other reasons, too. One being because it was a going-away present he had received from his civilian job when he was drafted, a gift his coworkers thought he could use in the army. It also served as a reminder of the life and a world he left behind; a life and a world he wanted to return to as soon and as safely as possible. The primary reason, though, was luck and maybe just knowing that if the inexpensive little flip-top lighter could make it through a one-year combat tour of duty in Vietnam, then so could he!

He kept the lighter, too, for the obvious reason. He smoked! It also came in handy for lighting the C-4 explosive used to heat C rations.

"Smoking's going to kill you, you know?" his buddy said, watching as Pilat took out a pack of cigarettes the night before another Thunder Run. The company had set up in a jungle perimeter, the tanks and tracks facing out, their weapons turned to the darkening wall of vegetation as dusk took over and the jungle became ominously quiet.

Pilat shrugged. "And this combat crap is healthy? Cigarettes settle my nerves."

"Sex does it for me." His buddy laughed. "The trouble

is, after these Thunder Runs, I'll probably race through that, too. A week after I get home, my wife will probably be calling me her 'Minute Man'!"

"Don't shoot until you see the whites of her thighs!" Pilat said, pulling out his lighter and unconsciously running his thumb over its top but stopping short of lighting the cigarette.

"Go ahead," his buddy said. "I'll take first shift." Guard duty was set up in rotational shifts, usually by rank and time in country. The NCOs on the track vehicles would get their choice, along with the vets, while the new guys would get the late-night or early-morning hours.

"You sure?"

Pilat's buddy nodded. "Smoking will kill you. I prefer to die in bed, thank you."

Pilat shook his head and smiled as he slid down the side of the M-113, walking toward the back of the vehicle where it was okay to light up. In the defensive perimeter, the modern-day wagon train of personnel carriers and tanks would shield the light and glow of the smokers from possible enemy snipers. The small perimeter was the soldiers' safe haven in the field, but a tentative one at best.

Other soldiers, not on guard duty, were eating C rations or cleaning weapons. Pilat had flipped the lid of the lighter with one quick flick and was about to thumb the flint to life when he stopped suddenly; something outside their perimeter *crack*ed as he and the others turned in instant recognition.

The shoulder-fired rocket-propelled grenade hit Pilat's track at its cupola. The explosion splashed fragments of metal, bone, and flesh into the evening.

As the Big Red One's mechanized grunts immediately

returned fire to beat back the attack, Pilat scrambled for his rifle. He was firing as he climbed back to the top of the track, where he found his buddy—or what was left of him.

"Oh God!" he cried, trying to pull the carcass back to safety while firing into the jungle. By then, the attack had faltered, and the enemy was retreating as the heavy machine guns pulverized the rain forest and the Viet Cong ranks with it.

Within minutes, it was over. There was no reasonable or decent explanation why some people had died and others were spared. Later, when there was time to reflect on how it all unfolded, when his hands had finally stopped shaking and he could steady the lighter's flame below his cigarette with both hands, there was only co-incidence to point to or fate to blame it on, again.

But for Darrel Pilat, there remained only the lingering belief that his safety was somehow connected to his lighter. As the war wore on and the firefights started and stopped with their usual frequency, and again and again he had been spared, his theory grew with significance.

As his tour of duty wound down, the only comfort he had was that the lighter was still intact. Its luck was holding true. From the jungle, he was lifted out to the di-vision's rear area to begin his out-processing. The night before he left for Long Binh, the base camp was shelled and mortared. Pilat lit up a cigarette and smoked it qui-etly, running his thumb over the lighter's case, knowing that, in spite of the explosions, he was going to be okay.

When the cigarette was done, he pulled out another, along with his lighter, but that time, when he flicked it open, the lighter broke in his hands.

"No big deal, man," another soldier said. He offered Pilat a light with his own lighter. "No big deal at all," he said. But Pilat wasn't listening. In the distance, the booming thunder of a monsoon echoed across the countryside.

There were still hours to go before he boarded the airplane that would take him home, and he could feel the panic rising in his chest, growing and drowning out the war and the weather. He stared at the broken lighter; it was a big deal, bigger than the other soldier or anyone else could ever imagine.

LIONS AND TIGERS AND FLARES, OH MY!

Imagine visiting a zoo only to realize once you're there that there are no bars or cages for any of the animals, no trenches or fences for the elephants, tigers, and water buffalo, no glass partitions for the monkeys, birds, lizards, and deadly snakes, and no way out for 365 days. Now throw into the zoo an opposing army that wants to kill you. Welcome to a typical jungle patrol.

In the animal kingdom usurping the
throne is usually called lunch.
—PETE DELANEY

It sounded like a woman's terrified scream, and it brought the five-man LRRP/Ranger patrol immediately up and ready as they turned their weapons in the direction of the peacock screaming in the distance.

After a few tense moments when the team leader was convinced it was, in fact, a peacock, and thinking about how much he hated Vietnam, he let the team ease back into relax mode. If it wasn't the swarms of malaria-carrying mosquitoes hovering and harassing you at night, the occasional cobra that would scare the crap out of you when it reared back and flared its hood, a tiger's low, sustained growl that kept you wide awake all night, or the sleep-jarring, shrieking birds, then it was the elephants, water buffalo, crocodiles, bears, leopards, spiders, centipedes, or cat-size frigging rats!

In the early morning, the jungle was still bathed in twilight, and the team wouldn't begin to saddle up and move for an hour or so, until the sun forced its way through the treetops.

The job of the LRRP/Rangers was long-range patrol, which simply meant that a specially picked and intensively trained five- or six-man team of soldiers would be inserted into enemy-held territory to find and observe enemy forces and gather intelligence information for the divisions, brigades, and field force units the teams served.

When all went according to plan, the small, special-operations patrols would go about their business undetected. When things went wrong, they went wrong quickly, and the LRRP team fought desperately to stay alive.

Just then, the patrol was going as planned. Sort of. They had spent the previous twelve hours watching a small jungle trail the Viet Cong had used as an infiltration route into Binh Long Province. So far there'd been nothing except a few grunts from several monkeys high up in the trees, an occasional croak from an unseen lizard, and the god-awful mating scream of the peacock.

The team leader sighed. If all was well within the animal and reptile world, then all was well for the team. But not all was well with his bladder. He had to urinate.

"Cover me," he said to the rear scout, who nodded. "I need to take a piss."

The team leader put his rifle down, rose to his knees, unbuttoned his jungle fatigue trousers, and as he took out his penis, it was his turn to scream.

"Aiiieee!" he wailed, falling back on his heels, staring in horror at his crotch. The rest of the team was suddenly back up, covering the jungle, searching for the obvious threat. Frightened birds nesting above shrieked and then fluttered noisily through the trees. Fear and adrenaline raced through the patrol because whatever the problem was it was close and personal. The rear scout was at the team leader's side, dragging him down while searching for puncture wounds. Jesus! Did he get bit by a snake while he was taking a piss?

"*Get it off! Get it off!*" the team leader yelled to the soldier.

The rear scout turned his focus to the team leader's penis and saw a finger-size, greenish-brown leech had crawled up the team leader's pant leg during the night, found the warm crotch, and attached itself to the side of the man's penis. The leech was thick with blood, and the penis was swollen and badly discolored. The rear scout knew garlic and silver crosses worked with vampires, but what the hell worked with bloodsuckers?

"Get it off!" the team leader yelled again, getting to his feet while covering his crotch with his hands. With his pants down around his ankles, the team leader was struggling to keep his balance. Grace or decorum were definitely out of the picture.

"Get it off!"

The rear scout took a look at the team leader and back at the man's unit and shook his head. "No!" he said, adamantly. "I ain't touching your dick! Uh-uh."

"Lemmee see," the team's medic said, moving the rear scout aside while the assistant team leader and the radioman covered the surrounding jungle. If the Viet Cong hadn't known they were there before the team leader's scream, they knew it now.

"It's just a leech," the team medic said, pulling out a survival knife and rooting around his aid bag for a bag of salt.

"What are you doing with *that*?" the team leader asked, staring at the knife blade.

"I'm going to pour some salt on the leech and remove it."

"Not with the knife, you aren't! Get away from me!"

"It's no big deal . . ."

"It's *my* dick! Fuck you! Get away from me!" the team leader cried, scrambling back to his rucksack and finding what he was looking for. Carefully, with one hand, he lifted his penis and held it steady, shuddering as the leech shifted with the motion. The team leader lit the match and placed it on the back of the leech. The greenish-brown lump began to shiver and tremble until it finally arched in pain, releasing its bite. The LRRP flicked it off. A small, steady stream of blood flowed from the puncture wounds down the shaft of his penis, and dripped to the jungle floor. He shuddered involuntarily.

"You're going to need a bandage," said the medic, holding out a bandage and strip of tape. "The bleeding won't stop for a while."

"Not now," said the team leader, weakly.

The side of his penis was green and yellow and throbbed with a thousand pinpricks. He still had to pee, so he came back up on his knees and urinated forcefully, wincing in pain as he propped himself up with his M-16 while trying to apply pressure to the wound to stop the bleeding. Urinating was a slow, painful ordeal, and when he had finished, he took the bandage from the medic, wrapped his penis, and then applied the tape. The blood was already seeping through the bandage when he placed the injured member back in his jungle fatigue trousers and buttoned up. Once done, he made certain his pant legs were securely tucked into his boots. Bending at the waist to tie the pant legs caused a shooting pain from his penis up through his stomach and spine and into the base of his brain where it registered smartly and forced his eyes to shut in reaction.

If he was lucky, the small wound wouldn't get infected. But a simple scratch in the jungle could easily swell and fester to the point where the treatment would require antibiotics, more clean bandages, and coming to terms with excruciating pain. He'd have to get the wound examined at the aid station, but he didn't welcome the idea.

"Saddle up!" the assistant team leader said to the others. "We've got to get out of here. This place sucks."

The team leader winced, uncertain which hurt worse, the leech bite or the sarcasm. The muffled laughter from the rest of the team wasn't helping his self-esteem much either. God, he hated Vietnam. He really, really hated the place!

"I KILLED HO CHI MING"

In The Emperor's New Clothes, *it took a little boy to point out that the emperor wasn't wearing anything before the rest of the king's subjects realized the folly of the event. The people saw what they wanted to see regardless of reality. In this account from an alleged Green Beret, the holes in the fabric begin to show early on.*

It is always the best policy to speak the truth, unless, of course, you are an exceptionally good liar.
—JEROME K. JEROME

It was a weekend military show in Las Vegas, Nevada, and the crowded exhibition hall was filled with thousands of veterans and enthusiasts.

Many of the veterans meandering through the maze of displays, exhibition booths, and sales tables were dressed in the usual array of uniform parts, T-shirts, and sweat shirts emblazoned with legends and logos of military units. Thanks to Hollywood and movies like *Rambo*, *Navy SEALs*, and John Wayne's *The Green Berets*, the most popular of the designs were those of the army Rangers, United States Marine Corps Force Recon, Special Forces, and the navy SEALs, and they were there in abundance.

Since the mid to late eighties, an unusual phenomenon had been noticed: people who had never served in the military were declaring themselves to be Vietnam veterans, and real veterans were claiming to have served with elite units to enhance their service. One study noted that while thirty-five hundred soldiers were said to have served as LRRP/Rangers over the course of the war, more than five thousand veterans have since claimed to have served in LRRP/Ranger units. So it was no surprise when attendees to the weekend event showed up with hats, berets, T-shirts, and uniform jackets bearing logos or patches of elite units.

There were also a few attendees dressed in battle-dress uniforms of foreign military units, including those of the French Foreign Legion.

Behind the Lines magazine, the journal of U.S. Military Special Operations, had set up a booth at the show, and its executive editor, Gary Linderer, had invited its editors and contributors to attend. Among those at the booth during the long weekend were Gary Linderer, Kenn Miller, Reynel Martinez, Larry Chambers, Greg Walker, Doc Norton—all veterans who'd served in elite units—and others who were talking with veterans, answering questions, telling war stories, or signing their books.

As the magazine's "humorist," I was there as well, looking for unusual stories. One advantage of events like that is that I knew I wouldn't have to search very hard to find them. That time I was lucky because the story came to me.

"Magazine, huh?" one visitor asked, stopping in front of the table and checking out the booth and staring at a stack of back issues of *Behind the Lines*.

"Yes, we are," I said. "Here! Take a complimentary copy." I handed him one.

Linderer and Martinez were taking a coffee break while Kenn Miller and I manned the booth. However, much of Miller's attention was taken up by a Taiwanese film crew whose members were surprised and pleased to find an American who was able to answer their questions in their native tongue. Two of them, in fact; Miller is fluent in several Chinese dialects.

"What do you do at the magazine?" the visitor asked, studying my name tag.

"A senior editor," I said, "which just means I'm old. You a vet?"

"Nam," he replied. I nodded.

He was overweight and balding and wore what hair remained in a ponytail beneath a battered green beret. "Special Forces, huh?" I said. This time he nodded.

"You with the Group or SOG?" I asked.

He shook his head. "Green berets," he said. I sighed.

He was dressed in jeans, frayed jungle boots, a T-shirt that read HONK IF YOU'RE HORNY, and a jungle fatigue shirt with a variety of patches sewn on the sleeves. There were two colorful rows of combat ribbons that said he had seen combat but that he didn't know which order it came in. That was his first mistake. The red-white-and-blue-striped Silver Star award was placed after an Air Medal, below a Purple Heart, and next to a Good Conduct Medal. His Silver Star award also had a V device indicating that the award was for valor, which was another mistake, because the Silver Star is awarded for gallantry, which in the military scope of things ranks a step above valor. It is not awarded with a V device.

A blue-and-white Combat Infantryman's Badge was pinned just above the ribbons with a flat silver oblong badge. The flat badge had a triangle in its center, and I didn't recognize it at first. Then I smiled seconds later, realizing that I had seen it on the uniforms of the officers who manned the bridge on the television series *Star Trek,* either generation.

The combat patch on his right sleeve was an olive drab subdued MAC-V insignia, while a Special Forces arrowhead patch was sewn on the left sleeve. On one shirt jacket pocket was a death's-head skull; an ace of spades was sewn on the opposite pocket. A number of Vietnam War–related pins were spread out across the pocket flaps and lapels like shrapnel from an exploding surplus store, but it was his green beret that caught most of my attention.

The weathered beret had a Special Forces insignia, a French paracommando crest, and the flat-black rank pin of a Marine lance corporal. The crests, patches, other insignia, and beret were an unusual mix of services, units, and time warps. It was happening again.

Earlier that morning while Linderer, Miller, and I were seated at the table at the booth, a man approached wearing an army fatigue shirt with a generic 75th Infantry Ranger scroll on the right shoulder as a combat patch. Since there wasn't a division or field force patch beneath it, there was no way of knowing which company he had served in during the war.

"I was a Ranger in Nam," he said. Linderer and Miller looked up.

"Who were you with?" asked Linderer, meaning which unit and where. It was the standard greeting ritual veterans go through with other veterans to establish common ground and a bond.

"The Second Batt," said the man. "The Second Batt" meant the 2d Ranger Battalion.

Linderer smiled. Miller, on the other hand, was sneering, as I pointed out that there wasn't a 2d Ranger Battalion in Vietnam.

"In fact, the battalions didn't exist back then, just companies," Linderer added, smiling.

Miller smiled, too, but it was the deranged grin of a pit bull sizing up a poodle. "You worthless piece of shit! I ought to cut your legs off," he said, with as much diplomacy as he could muster.

Kenn Miller is one of only a handful of LRRP/Rangers to have served two and a half years with the 101st Airborne in behind-the-lines combat. He has little patience for "wanna-be" elite combat veterans and a pathological disgust for those who'd wear a 75th Ranger combat patch pretending to have earned it.

Linderer was still shaking his head in disgust as the make-believe LRRP/Ranger veteran quickly excused himself, realizing that he had somewhere else to be.

Throughout the previous evening and much of that morning, we had encountered other such "make-believe" veterans, including a French Foreign Legionnaire who couldn't speak French, a navy SEAL or two who couldn't remember which team they served with, and other pretend Rangers who wore the 75th Ranger scroll company patch over the wrong division or field force patch. So when this latest "Green Beret" turned up, not knowing what "Group" or "SOG" were, I knew it was starting all over again.

"I got a good story for you," he said while I nodded. "I don't know if it has been declassified yet," he said, and then shrugged, adding in conspiratorial tones, "Who knows? It probably never will be."

"So, who did you serve with?" I asked, beginning the process by working through the basics.

"Special Forces," he said, "Black Ops." I nodded again, taking out my notebook and jotting that down.

"Not SOG, huh?" He offered a confused look in return. SOG was the acronym for the Studies and Observations Group, a pleasant-sounding innocuous title for some very unpleasant secret missions. Since Hollywood hadn't discovered SOG yet, back then the general public knew little about it.

I scanned the rest of the man's makeshift uniform again. It took a few seconds to realize he wasn't wearing jump wings; the standard U.S. Army parachutist badge. This was like a nun without her habit, a sheriff without a badge or, say, Vegas without an Elvis impersonator.

"So, where did you serve?" I asked, giving my best *60 Minutes* Mike Wallace stare. It was a shame I didn't have a loud stopwatch.

"Where?" he echoed.

I nodded. "Yeah. Which corps area? When were you in country?"

"All over," he said, cryptically evading the question. "I did a few tours." Then he came back at me with more immediate concerns. "So how much can you pay for the story?" he asked.

I smiled. "Complimentary copies, a few free magazines, if it's published."

"That isn't very much," he said.

"No kidding," I said. Those who don't write for a living always believe those who do make a whole shitload of money. Sometimes, I even show my friends my bank balance just to make them feel better about their own lives. I've considered showing them my royalty checks, but their laughter would only hurt my feelings and what was left of my pride. Sometimes I wonder if I should have taken up plumbing.

Mulling it over, the Special Forces *Star Trek* veteran reluctantly decided it still might be worth his time. "I just want people to know the real story. That's all," he said. "I want to get it off my chest."

"Get what off of your chest?" I asked. He was quiet for a long moment.

"I killed Ho Chi Ming," he said, finally.

"Who?" I asked, not quite believing what I thought I had heard. Maybe it was the way he mumbled or maybe the noise in the convention hall or maybe it was something else entirely.

"The Vietnamese leader?"

"You mean Ho Chi Minh?" I asked.

He just nodded. "Yeah, that's what I said."

"And you killed him?"

The storyteller nodded again. "Yeah, on a secret mission. Black Ops. We were a special hit team doing a job for the CIA. There were only three of us. The other two are dead now. I'm the only one left."

I studied his face as he told his tale, thinking he had to be ten years younger than I, which meant that at the time of Ho Chi Minh's death in 1969, the storyteller would have been all of fourteen.

"I thought Ho Chi Minh died of a heart attack," I said, knowing it was a reasonable enough statement since it was in most of the history books and encyclopedias. Sometimes my remarkable interviewing skills even amaze me, but then, I've always done well with the obvious.

"That's what they wanted everyone to believe!"

Some days aren't as interesting as others, but this one was beginning to show promise. "So, how did you do it?" I asked.

"Huh?"

"How did you and your two teammates do it?"

The storyteller looked around to see if anyone was listening, and when he was certain there was more interest than just me, he increased his volume. He went into a ridiculous story about it being a suicide mission that the

CIA wrote off. How they were parachuted over the jungle base where Ho was guarded by a couple hundred special Russian soldiers, and how the three snuck up on the North Vietnamese leader like they had been trained.

"Just you and the two other Americans?"

"Uh-huh. And while they kept the guards busy, I snuck in and blew him away, man."

"Ho Chi Ming?" I asked again, just to be certain I had heard him correctly. "And you reported back where?"

"What?"

"Not what. Where? As in, what base? Nha Trang? Da Nang? Star Fleet Command? Where?"

"What's that supposed to mean?"

"It means that I'd like to look at a copy of your DD214 if you have one on you," I replied, asking about the army discharge form that officially outlined his service. Well, at least the major points anyway. The form contains the duty stations, service codes, years of service, tours of overseas duty, schools and training, awards, and other information outlining an individual's service. While there were, in fact, secret or special operations groups sneaking and peeking during the Vietnam War, a G.I.'s DD214 would point in that direction also.

"It's been sanitized," he said.

"Sanitized?"

"Erased to cover it up."

With even a basic understanding of military administration—the kind any literate soldier would take away from an enlistment—the codes on a DD214 could easily be deciphered. For example, a soldier who was parachute qualified and who had served as a buck sergeant (E-5) in an infantry unit would carry a military occupational specialty code of 11B4P. The DD214 wouldn't list every duty station, but it would at least point you in the right direction, and any other questions concerning units, training, awards and decorations, education, time in service, time overseas, and even the last duty assignment would be answered.

"There's no record of the mission anywhere, man," he said, more than a little annoyed by my line of questioning. "I told you, it was Black Ops. Top secret! It isn't in my military records."

"Okay, then how about telling me which Special Forces group you were with? And when you served with it? And maybe a few names, like your commanding officer, sergeant major, or team sergeant or anyone else who I can check with to verify any of your story." The nice thing about BTL magazine is that it is a network of *hooahs!*, real-life special-operations types who, if they didn't have the answers within reach, knew how to put you in touch with those who did. Mr. Disney was right. It's a small world after all.

"Fuck it! I don't need this shit!" the visitor said, irritated by my asking for some sources.

"Neither do the rest of us Nam vets, sport, the real Vietnam veterans. So right now, I'd settle for your driver's license to check your birth date to make sure that the Special Forces or the CIA didn't recruit you out of junior high school for your remarkably daring deed."

"You saying I'm lying?"

I grinned. "Yeah, and badly, too," I added. "So how do you spell your name anyway, because I want to make sure I get this story right. It's a good one!"

"Fuck you!" he said, walking away.

"Is that with one F or two?" I said, calling after him, only he kept on walking. God, I hate those French names.

BUYING INTO HISTORY

"You know what these are?" the new guy said excitedly to the veteran as they came in from a pass into town. It was the new guy's first visit, and the veteran was showing him around the street markets and bars.

"Yeah. Ho Chis," the veteran said. "Tire-tread sandals. Where'd you get them?"

"One of the street vendors. Pretty cool, huh?"

The veteran nodded, studying the crude sandals that were made from the tread of car tires. Rubber strips from bicycle tubes served as the straps. "Depends on how much you spent on them."

"Fifty dollars MPC! Why?" MPC were military payment certificates and, judging from the expression on the veteran's face, the new guy could see that his buddy thought it was way too much.

"For a pair of Ho Chi Minh sandals?"

"Yeah! A pair of *his* sandals!"

The veteran studied the new guy for a moment and then laughed. "You dumbshit! They're not Ho Chi *Minh*'s sandals. They're called Ho Chi Minh sandals because the Viet Cong wear them. Hell, these aren't even Viet Cong sandals anyway; these are made from jeep tires."

DISSOLVE TO BLACK

It's prejudice, blatant prejudice. That's all it is. Plain and simple. Hollywood hates Jorgensons.

It's true. They do. What's more, it's more sinister than that. They want us dead. In fact, they've been killing us off for years. The first time I noticed they were out to get us was when I was a twelve-year-old, watching an old John Wayne movie on TV. The movie *The Flying Leathernecks* was about Marine Corps pilots during World War II.

In one scene, the Duke walks into a briefing room, throws down his leather flying cap after a tough combat mission, and says, "Well, they got Jorgenson."

At the time, I thought nothing of it other than, "Hey! That's my name, too!" It was no big thing then, especially to a twelve-year-old whose name was something of an oddity in southern Catholic school circles anyway. I recall one instance when a nun walked down the rows of desks offering comfort to those of us in the classroom. Sort of.

"John? You're named for St. John? Mary? You're named for the Blessed Virgin, and Kregg with a K . . . hmm? You're named for a heathen barbarian."

The only "Jorgensen" anyone had heard of then was Christine Jorgensen, the man who had a sex change. It was no relation, but I was constantly ribbed about it anyway, so the movie reference to a pilot, especially a Marine Corps combat pilot, was really something. Sure, they killed him off, but it was just one good reference in one movie, right?

Of course, in another one of his movies, *The Searchers,* John Wayne was riding after a group of marauding Indians who had kidnapped a woman. The Indians cut a wide swath over the territory, and we soon learn that they wiped out an entire family over "yonder."

"Well, they got the Jorgensons," mutters the Duke.

We're not talking one this time, but an entire family.

I wrote it off then as coincidence—that is, until the movie *Rambo: First Blood Part II* when Hollywood eliminated another one of my relatives.

It's the scene where Sylvester Stallone's in a cave sewing up a wound with a bent nail and fishing line, or something. Anyway, his old commander, played by Richard Crenna, gets on a radio and begins calling out Rambo's old teammates and guess who's there? That's right, another Jorgenson, to which Stallone replies, "They're all dead!"

Dead? Did he say "Dead"? Why yes, he did. Now maybe in Copenhagen or Oslo that might not be such a big thing, but in Hollywood it's termination with extreme prejudice.

Don't believe me? Well, let's cut again to the movie *For the Boys* with Bette Midler and James Caan. There we learn that Midler's son is an officer in Vietnam, and she's worried about him. In fact, we find her frantic in her kitchen, watching a news clip of a soldier who had been shot and was being helped back by a medic. She's troubled by this, but then so was I, because the trouble *here* is that it's real footage of the war, with *me* getting shot. It was taken from a CBS news clip when the newspeople joined our platoon for a patrol along the Cambodian border. In it, I get shot, helped back by the medic and another soldier, interviewed, and then whisked away by a medevac helicopter.

"No big thing," you say? Actually it wasn't, unless you consider that they only show me getting shot and dragged back while the narrator on the TV *in the movie* adds, "And the soldier later died."

Died? I didn't die.

I first learned about this from one of my daughters who saw the movie, saw the film clip in the movie, and called, crying, saying that the movie said I died. "No, honey," I assured her. "It's only my deodorant."

The news clip has been used in a documentary about the war, used to sell a Time-Life series of books on the Vietnam war, and on *60 Minutes* as background footage when they were talking about combat, or in one instance, a veteran who had murdered a woman and stabbed her friend. After that airing or one that involved "trip-wire" or allegedly crazy veterans, I received calls from friends and relatives asking me how I was doing just before they asked if I had, say, a chain saw and a hockey mask in my garage and would I please lock them up.

Of course, not all my friends call to ask how I'm doing. When Jerry Boyle, author of *Apache Sunrise*, sees that clip, he usually calls and laughs. Jerry and I served together in the same unit in Vietnam. He was a gunship pilot, and I was an infantry squad leader. He calls me "grunt," and I call him "rotorhead."

"Hey, grunt, I just saw you get shot again," he'll say in his gravelly voice.

"Time-Life selling their books again?"

"Something like that. Hey, I have a question for you."

"Okay, what is it?"

"You've been shot what? One thousand times or so now?"

"On TV, yeah about that. Why?"

"Huh? You'd think you would have learned to duck about now?"

If that's not bad enough, then consider that the transition has carried over from Hollywood to the literary world. In Thom Jones's collection of short stories, *The Pugilist at Rest*, a National Book Award nominee, Jones writes about a good Marine and a bad Marine in Vietnam. The good Marine is a Jorgenson, so guess what happens to him? You got it, he dies. Deader than disco. Sure, and you thought I was paranoid.

Don't miss Kregg P. J. Jorgenson's true story of ambushed LRRPs and their Apache Troop rescuers in the NVA-infested jungles of Cambodia:

MIA RESCUE

LRRPs in Cambodia

---

by
Kregg P. J. Jorgenson

Published by Ballantine Books.
Available at bookstores everywhere.